Allegheny River Rails to Trails Guide

Written by CJ Grant
Photography by CJ Grant

Edited by Nancy Whyte
Photo Editing by Mike Stone

This book is dedicated to Patricia Milford, one of my dearest friends. She stood by my side unconditionally through the deaths of both of my sisters, my mother and my father. Without her strength and support through those time, I'm not sure these guides would be possible.

Table of Contents

Acknowledgements

Of all the words written within these guides, these are the most difficult and the most important within the books. I owe so much to many people for their help with the completion of this long process.

First, I need to thank my editor, Nancy Whyte, for the endless hours of pouring over my dribble and making me sound intelligent before we went to print. Her almost daily emails encouraged me through some of the darkest times while dredging through the writing process.

Without the complete sponsorship of Otto Schiberl Jr. a.k.a. Buster and Vicki Whitmer, this project would not have started either. They generously provided the bicycles, gasoline money, expense money, and publication funds to complete these projects. I cannot thank them enough for their dedication to helping the community and faith in my ability to put out these guides in a professional manner.

The guides required an extreme amount of research and fact verification too. It was imperative that the information provided within the pages was completely accurate. In order to verify my findings along the trail, I asked Jim Holden, the president of Allegheny Valley Trail Association, to assist in the editing process. With his assistance and the wonderful suggestions from Debra Frawley, we accomplished this feat.

Jake Weiland, the park manager at Oil Creek State Park was also extremely helpful in the process. With his guidance and the assistance of the other park employees, we developed an accurate and informative guide for that park.

The research required many hours and days of biking and hiking alone on the vast miles of trails within this guide. When I originally accepted the project, I feared in the back of my mind that I could not do it. Luckily, my great nephew, Dakota Peterson, was staying at my house for the summer and started the trail riding expedition with me. Through him, I gained the courage to face my fears and came to the realization that I could continue hiking and biking the trails without him.

As I mention within the guides, I had a few friends that mustered up the courage to ride with me occasionally. I owe them thanks too. Among them are Sandra Mulvey, Shawnee Mulvey, Jamie and Eric, and Jim my talkative, diehard, fellow biker.

I need to thank Dave Staab and Brad Rapp at *The Progress News* for their patience with my ceaseless questions about setting up files, inserting photos into text, and assisting in making the finished project look professional.

My final thanks you goes back to childhood. Without my mother's encouragement to go return to school to be a writer in my thirties, I would not be sitting here now. I remember coming in from playing and always having a fantastic tale to tell her when I walked in the door. I did it to amuse her. She listened with a huge smile and occasional laughter as my creativity developed. I had no idea she was grooming me to be the writer that I am today. Even beyond the grave, I believe she is still listening to my stories with a smile that lights up my days even at this moment.

Introduction

I started hiking in the woods of Northwestern Pennsylvania when I was four years old. My mother told me that on a regular basis, I would take our dog Lassie into the woods and follow a stream not far from our farmhouse. I fondly recall some of those times as if they were yesterday.

Of those innocent days, I particularly remember one quite vividly. I followed the stream and sat at my favorite spot, where the water flowed over a series of rocks forming a small waterfall. I sat there wondering why everyone built their houses on the roads when they could have instead built a house out there by the waterfall. Then I wished for such a house.

God granted me that wish. For nine years I have lived along the Allegheny River, and yes, during most seasons, behind my house there is a gushing waterfall. As I sit here writing this passage, it is just after Christmas, and I am watching an osprey soar over the tops of the huge trees that flourish along the steep river bank. And, as an adult, I still ponder why most people choose to live along a strip of asphalt instead of at the end of a dirt road surrounded by Nature's beauty.

There are endless astounding sights one can see along the Allegheny River if one just takes a moment to acknowledge the great gifts that our environment contains. This is one of the main reasons I have chosen to write this guide: to encourage others to visit the trails so that they, too, can be surrounded by the beauty and the wildlife that I am fortunate to witness on a daily basis.

As when I was a child hiking the railroad beds along the curvy river, the outdoors continue to beckon me. Since moving here, I continue to be humbled by my surroundings. I have photographed the environment and its wildlife extensively, and on every hike or bike ride, I am filled with an inner peace and I am always rewarded with constantly-changing displays of beauty.

In addition to encouraging others to witness the splendors of Nature while traveling along the trail, it is my hope that this guide will facilitate trail users to gain a better understanding of the Native Americans who once inhabited the area as well as to learn about and appreciate the significance of the region's oil heritage.

I also want to steer my reader through the trails so they may experience each section of the trail with a knowledgeable eye for what *they might encounter on each mile of this amazing trail system. Thus, while providing important information for trail users, I am called to share some of the memorable experiences I've accumulated while biking the miles of the Allegheny River Rails to Trails. Each time that I rode the sections of this trail, I saw different sights and discovered more of what it had to offer. This guide is a work in progress because the river that the trail follows, like life, continues to change. An accurate guide of what is to come can not be written. My goal is to enhance the trail user's adventures so they, too, can safely and enjoyably gather their own wealth of happy memories.*

What You Need to Know First

Whether you are experiencing the Allegheny Valley Rails to Trails for a family vacation or enjoy the trails on a daily basis, it is important to know how to safely use the trails. Because this guide is intended to be useful to anyone engaging in bicycling, boating, canoeing, camping, cross country running, cross-country skiing, fishing, horseback riding, jogging, kayaking, and roller-skating, knowing the safety rules for each sport is imperative before you begin the journey.

The trails sometimes present other issues that you must also be prepared for. Here is a brief guide of things you will need on the trail.

The Tunnels

Two of the major trails of the trail system, the Allegheny River Trail between Emlenton and Brandon and the Sandy Creek Trail, have long tunnels that you will need a flashlight to see your way safely through. These tunnels, cut by old steam shovels to facilitate railroad travel along the river, are astounding feats of construction and demonstrate the importance of the railroad during the days of the oil boom. However, the tunnels are long enough that they are very difficult to maneuver through without a self-supplied light. Even with a flashlight, it is advisable to walk one's bike through the tunnel instead of riding. Although the trails are level and smoothly paved, in the shadowed lighting it is easy to lose one's equilibrium and perhaps veer off the paved surface.

When heading out on any trail, it is always advisable to bring a flashlight just in case for some unforeseen reason you have to guide yourself out after dark. But you definitely need a flashlight in order to safely enjoy the tunnels. Going through these tunnels is an interesting experience you will not forget. So by no means avoid these trails: just remember to bring a flashlight so that you can pass through the tunnels safely.

Water

Most outdoor enthusiasts realize the importance of keeping oneself properly hydrated, and this trail system is so pretty that you will probably find yourself out there longer than you originally anticipated when starting your journey. The many benches, picnic areas, scenic overlooks, and historical landmarks will invite you to linger, and time will fly as you enjoy the remarkable scenery and wildlife along the miles of trails. Thus, make sure you bring along a sufficient supply of water. Regardless of whether it is winter or summer, our bodies constantly require an adequate supply of water. I recommend that you err on the side of caution and bring with you more water than you think you will need for your trek.

Food

The fresh air and scenic sights of the trail experience provide a wonderful setting for picnics. However, even if you are not planning on stopping for a picnic, you should always bring with you some type of high-energy food.

Like the Boy Scouts and Girl Scouts of America's motto, you should always "Be Prepared" when on the trail. Taking a candy bar or trail mix along with you even for a short ride is a good idea, and it is particularly important in case you travel farther than you had originally intended --- something easily done. Your blood sugar level may run low, and physically you will need the added boost to complete your journey safely and comfortably

First Aid Kit

Because stretches of the Allegheny Valley Trails system are very remote, when traveling along the trails, I highly recommend bringing along a first aid kit. Most of the trails stretch for many miles before encountering a town or even a house. Many travelers report that their cell phones don't have service along some sections of the trails. This remoteness is one of the trails' charms, but the isolation creates difficulties should you have a medical emergency.

Even though all the trails allow emergency access for vehicles, it might take a while to get to you. The trails are also so vast that some days you might only pass one or two people on the trail. Carrying a first aid kit in your pack only makes sense.

Layers

All of the trails in this system are along waterways, and hundreds of years ago these very waters carved deep valleys through the surrounding hills and mountains. Year-round these canyons and cliffs present unique backdrops for photographs and homes for some endangered species. In the summer, they provide plenty of cool shade on even the hottest, bright days. The trail between Franklin and Oil City is like this. It can be sunny and warm everywhere else, but in the shade of the high cliffs, a person may feel somewhat chilled.

It is always easier to shed clothes on the trail than to put them on. Either way, bring extra layers of clothing with you so that you can be comfortable should you need to add or subtract layers. After sunset, even in mid-summer, the air becomes cool along the water.

Side trails often entice users to venture off the paved path, and will often lead you to surprising wonders. However, they can also present additional hazards.

Many of the side trails lead to major attractions. Indian God Rock between Brandon and Belmar is one example. Since the 1700's, this site has attracted visitors. It is a very spiritual and sacred Native American site where petroglyphs testify to the existence of an ancient form of communication that still leaves its mark today. Anyone who travels along this extension of the trail system should definitely visit this historical site, but be forewarned that there is poison ivy growing all along the path leading down to the petroglyphs.

Poison Oak can also be found along many of the paved trails. If you have any intention of going off the paved trail --- and most of us will be tempted to do just that --- I suggest that you bring some long pants with you that you can slip on. It is well worth the extra little bit of weight in your pack if it prevents you from getting a rash.

Bug Repellent

Like every other part of North America, you will find bugs along the trails. Make sure you apply bug repellent before you head out on the trail, and take some with you just in case you are out longer than you expect and the first application wears off.

There is nothing worse than receiving an itchy bite when you are hours away from relief. Regardless, if you do get bitten by bugs, try not to scratch. While it may be difficult to do so, your best bet is to wait until you can use soap and cool water to thoroughly wash the bitten area. Scratching the itch may seem to bring temporary relief, but in reality only prolongs the itchy problem.

The Sticks

The entire Allegheny Valley trail system is well maintained, but old growth trees bank the trails. Especially after strong winds, sticks and occasionally limbs fall on the trail and can hinder your smooth passage. The small, thin sticks are usually easy to avoid, but be forewarned to use caution anyway: what appears to be a fallen twig may instead be something else.

The paved trail often attracts other visitors, like snakes, that enjoy basking in the sunlight and soaking up the heat emitted from the pavement on a sunny day. It is important to identify what you are encountering before you pass it and particularly important that you know what you're stepping on.

As in other parts of Pennsylvania, certain snakes are native to the areas through which the trails pass. While most of the snakes you might see are non-poisonous, the possibility exists of coming across a copperhead or timber rattler, both of which are extremely venomous. So, use common sense when enjoying all the activities that the trails encourage. Make sure that you always use caution to make sure that you can see what might be there before you take a step or reach.

Wildlife

One of the most enjoyable parts of this gorgeous trail system is the wildlife that inhabits the areas along the trails. Sometimes you'll be astounded by what you're fortunate enough to see. On of the most special to me along the Allegheny River is the not-so-rare occurrence of glancing up and seeing a bald eagle soaring gracefully above, majestically floating on the air currents

White-tailed deer are very common along all parts of the trails. In some areas, like the Emlenton to Rockland section of the trail, the deer seem almost unafraid of the trail user. If you are inconspicuous when traveling on the trail, sometimes the deer will run along the woods parallel with you as you travel, or even bed down within feet of you..

There is such a vast number of indigenous wildlife in along this trail system that you are likely to encounter some sort of animal or bird no matter where you trek. The most important thing to remember is that although these animals may appear cute and harmless, they are wild animals and not pets. For two important reasons, it is imperative that you never attempt to get close to or try to feed any animal you meet. First of all, the animal may bite or scratch you, either of which could cause severe injuries to you. Secondly, these animals' survival depends on them maintaining their natural instincts which includes fearing humans.

Black bears, although rarely seen, are also present in northwestern Pennsylvania. If you should encounter a bear along the trail, keep as far away from it as possible, and slowly get away as soon as you can. Black bears usually pose no threat to humans, but if you happen upon a bear with cubs, the defending mother can be extremely dangerous. Slowly move away in the opposite direction.

You will see or hear dozens of chipmunks and squirrels frolicking through the underbrush, and although these furry little creatures are cute, they can be hazardous if they jump out in front of you. Often chipmunks act like kamikaze pilots and almost as if they are playing a game, they seem to enjoy startling you with their sudden appearance. Do not try to guess the little playful creature's next move. It is best to slow down until it safely gets to the side of the trail.

Trail Etiquette

Everyone should be comfortable moving at his or her own pace when using the trails. Often, you will have to pass someone who is going slower or who has stopped along the side of the trail. Before overtaking someone, as a courtesy and safety precaution, always warn the person in front of you that you are going to pass on the left. Not doing so could result in a person accidentally veering directly into your path or surprise them so much that they have an accident. These trails are remote and often you will not encounter another rider for some time, and many bikes commonly ridden make almost no sound. With no hint or warning of another's approach, one can easily be startled.

The rule of thumb used on the trail system is always to warn someone of your approach by telling them you are passing on the left.

Quiet on the trail

If you are in a group, this can be very difficult --- there always seems to be at least on chatterbox in any collection of people --- but riding as quietly as possible when traveling along the trail has distinct benefits. When quiet, you will be able to see more wildlife.

Also, some trail users, seeking harmony with nature in a near-spiritual manner, may resent the intrusion of outside noise. Thus, when on the trail, as a common courtesy, try not to prevent others from hearing Nature's sounds.

Littering

The Allegheny Valley Rails to Trails are so well maintained that you will seldom see any type of litter along the way. Trail users respect the beauty of the area so much that they try to keep the area pristine. The common rule, like on every other trail, is to pack out what you pack in to an area. Most courteous trail users will even pick up any other litter they find along the trail.

The entire area that these trails encompass is gorgeous and pristine. It is our duty to keep it this way by behaving in ways that do not pollute the area with litter or foul the appearance in any way.

Graffiti

In the wilderness, graffiti is not a form of art: it is a selfish desecration of nature that obscures the true beauty of the natural environment. Fortunately, you will seldom see any graffiti; trail users appreciate the rock formations and recognize abandoned ruins as historical monuments. Many sites are also sacred Native American places, and disfiguring them ruins their remarkable significance.

Unfortunately, the tunnels have fallen victim to some graffiti. Aside from committing an illegal act --- and most trail users hope the guilty taggers will be caught and prosecuted --- those who deface such sites of historical importance ruin the historical significance and mar the beauty of the trail for future passers-by.

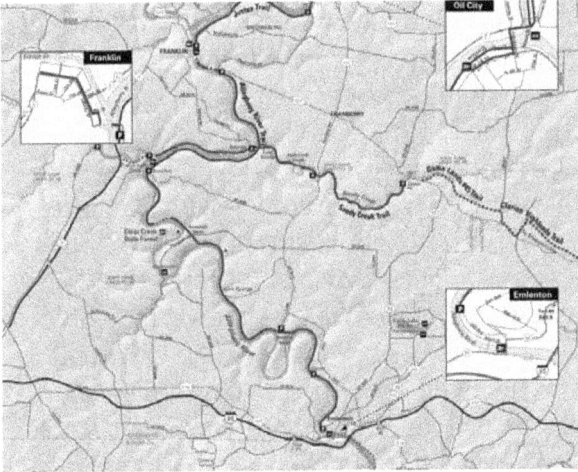

Map Generously Provided by Allegheny Valley Trails Association.

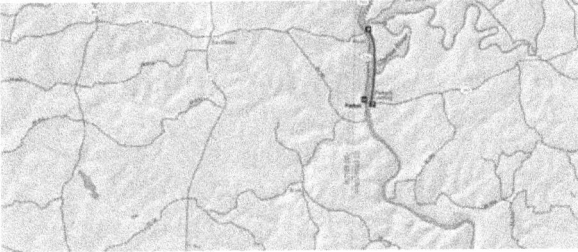

The Allegheny Valley Trails Association

The Allegheny Valley Trails Association (ATVA) is responsible for maintaining, developing, and regulating many of the miles of hiking, biking, canoeing, cross-country skiing, horseback riding, kayaking, jogging, and walking trails covered within these pages of this book. Formed in 1990 by two Clarion University professors, this association and the trails are the keystone to promoting eco-tourism through the wild and scenic northwest passage of the Allegheny

River including the waterways around the Oil Heritage region of Pennsylvania.

It all started with a simple suggestion from David Howes, a Geography professor at Clarion University after he participated in a bike race on Oil Creek along with his friend and fellow professor James Holden, who then was a Computer Science professor at the same school. "We had just finished the race at Oil Creek State Park, when Dave suggested that we should do something to develop the old abandoned rail road beds so that more people could enjoy the scenic beauty of our area. We both loved the idea, and enlisting the assistance of our spouses, the ATVA began with just the four of us. Dave was the president. His wife was the secretary; I was vice-president, and my wife was the treasurer," Jim recalled. "We thought it was an important contribution that we could do for our community. Everything developed from there."

This is a great illustration of how a simple idea, dedication to a great cause, and the desire to do something that helps others can create a miracle that touches the lives of thousands. What this group initiated became the most scenic stretch of paved level trails that can be found anywhere in America. It stretches from Titusville, PA, site of the world's first commercial oil well to Parker, "The Smallest City in United States".

"Our goal is to connect to other trail systems already in place or in the planning stages of development. The Allegheny River

Trails will eventually be part of a larger system of trails that travel south to Pittsburgh along the Allegheny River and continue north up to Erie. Eventually, we also hope to continue the trail system into New York," said Jim. "Plus, we want to develop a stringent maintenance plan to keep the trails in pristine condition."

The purpose that these four altruistic people developed for this trail is two-fold. The first is to improve the local economy for local residents by providing an opportunity for eco-tourism. The second is to provide recreational resources so that all people can enjoy the wild and scenic Allegheny River region. Through promoted development, the trails provide the means for everyone to enjoy recreational opportunities along the Allegheny River and surrounding area. The trails also provide the chance to experience the historic significance of this area.

Jim is now the president of AVTA. Dave is still a key player; he compiles the information and prepares the documents necessary to obtain grants that are crucial to the continued existence of this non-profit organization. The funding used to maintain and enhance this pristine series of trails comes from AVTA's annual membership dues. While there is never any cost for anyone to use the trails, the easily-affordable membership dues of AVTA are much needed and thoroughly appreciated. A single membership is only $20.00, and for just $25.00 a year, an entire family can join the association. At such reasonable rates, everyone is encouraged to join.

There are several benefits to becoming a member of this great association, but perhaps the most significant is the knowledge that you are helping to preserve and protect a beautiful and historically-rich segment of our nation's past. Along each trail are markers that explain the historic significance of individual locations including Drake's Well, the world's first commercially drilled oil well, and the once heavily-populated oil boom city of Parker which, despite its drastic reduction in population has ever-since maintained its city charter, as well as evidence of the Native Americans who originally inhabited the region..

Through the membership fees, the AVTA maintains the trails. They marker plaques providing historical information. They have placed many picnic tables and benches along the trails. Because the AVTA actually owns much of the land that the trails pass through, the association is responsible for paying taxes and buying insurance. The association produces publications that promote this unspoiled trail system. Members' dues help meet these expenses.

Members of the ATVA receive newsletters that report the latest developments and plans discussed at the bimonthly meetings. Association members are invited to attend these private meetings and to become more involved by sharing their voice and talents.

To develop the trail further, in the near future, the ATVA plans to continue the trail from Parker to West Monterey. After that, the trail will then extend to Upper Hilldale. At that point, the next fifty miles of what was once railroad bed along the Allegheny River is owned by another organization.

Because of the philanthropic dedication of a few great people who are responsible for beginning the ATVA, many of the towns that went from "Boom to Bust" after the first discoveries of oil in our area will now have the potential to revive economically due to the influx of people using the trail.

Please consider becoming a member of the ATVA. You are encouraged to join and become a part of this important endeavor. For more information, visit ATVA's website: http://www.atva-trails.org   The membership application is also listed on this informative site. Just print the simple membership form out and send to:

Allegheny Valley Trails Association
Box 264
Franklin, PA 16323

You may also contact **Ms. Debra Frawley**, Regional Greenways Coordinator for more information by phone. The number is **(814) 432-4476 Ext 121.**

Franklin

Although moderate in size, the city of Franklin has a small-town feel to it, and additionally it possesses significant historical appeal. Because of its important location at the confluence of French Creek and the Allegheny River, the history of the city of Franklin, named in 1795 to honor the great inventor and patriot Benjamin Franklin, is one of the most well-documented in Pennsylvania.

Native Americans were originally drawn to this strategic location and settled there. Later, early traders established markers here, too, until the French claimed the area in 1749 and ousted the early entrepreneurs. After news of the French expansion traveled to colonial governments, George Washington was sent to the area in 1753 to warn the French that they had encroached on British land. In his journal, he wrote an exciting account of this journey. A full version of this early expedition as it was originally published is available at http://www.earlyamerica.com/earlyamerica/milestones/journal/journaltext.html.

In this diary of his adventure through the Ohio River Valley, Washington refers to Franklin as Venango. This small historic city of Franklin is now the county seat of Venango County.

After the visit from George Washington, the French did not leave the area. Instead, the French built Fort Machault on the site. Eventually, though, the French abandoned the area to defend their Fort Niagara in the north. Before they left, the French burned Fort Machault so that it could not be utilized by the British. Soon after, the British took control of the area and built Fort Venango at the location. However, that fort was conquered by Native Americans in 1763 during Pontiac's Uprising, and the entire British garrison was massacred.

Manifest destiny prevailed, however, and the Allegheny River – French Creek location became more popular; at the time, the most direct route from the Great Lakes to the Mississippi River was actually via French Creek. Lacking the roads so commonplace today, in those days water was one of the easiest ways to travel, and colonial forces built Fort Franklin upon the site in 1787.

After Colonel Edwin Drake drilled the first commercial oil well nearby in nearby Titusville in 1859, Franklin's economy boomed with oil money, and many of the architectural marvels built using that newly-acquired wealth still stand today. Nothing illustrates this better than taking a walking tour through Franklin's quaint streets; one will view over twenty different types of styles of architecture that were popular during that era. A map of this tour is available at: http://www.ci.franklin.pa.us/photo_gallery_pix/map.jpg.

Franklin boats that it is a Bicycle-Friendly city. On Franklin's homepage at http://www.franklinpa.gov/, there is a map available, which offers an outlined path of this section. This makes it easy for visitors staying locally in Franklin to access the Samuel Justis Trail and the Allegheny River Trail without using motorized vehicles. In addition, on this website you can easily find places to stay, a list of museums in the area, and a directory for dates of the many festivals that the city of Franklin offers throughout the year.

The confluence of the two great waterways makes Franklin a popular destination for anyone who enjoys kayaking or canoeing. Whether going out on the Allegheny River or French Creek, the trip is guaranteed to be memorable. French Creek is a major tributary to the Allegheny, and traveling its shallow, rocky bed makes a great adventure even for beginning kayakers or canoers. It is also one of the cleanest watersheds east of the Mississippi River. The biodiversity in the clear waters is immense. French Creek alone hosts 80 different species of fish and 26 different species of mussels. Many of the fish and mussels are on the endangered list like the northern riffle shell and club shell along with the sand darter and spotted dotter. Many of these endangered species exist only in this watershed. Each of these species requires clean water to survive, and both French Creek and the Allegheny River harbor these endangered species.

The cleanliness of the waters also attracts a wide variety of wildlife. Both the bald eagle and the otter require clean waters for hunting. Thanks in great part this environment, both are repopulating the area at an amazing rate.

In 1992, the Allegheny River was designated as a National Wild and Scenic River, and because of that classification, the banks of the shores from Kinzua Dam to Emlenton are protected from most development. This makes for amazing water tours that lead you through vast areas of undeveloped pristine forests.

Franklin Canoe and Kayak Livery

Outdoor Allegheny River Services, OARS, is a reputable company for canoe and kayak rentals on both the Allegheny River and French Creek, and they offer competitive rates with a variety of extended overnight drop-off and pickup locations. They also have paddle and pedal trips available; you can paddle down river to a designated spot and ride your bicycle back to the original point. Your bike is transported for you to the meeting point. This makes for a great day trip that provides enjoyment of being on the water and pedaling along the banks through pristine wilderness areas. This facility is open 7 days a week and they also have primitive camping sites available. You can research OARS online for prices, trip planning, etc. at http://www.oarsontheallegheny.com/about_frenchcreek.html, or contact them by phone at 814-388-9122.

Franklin Bicycle Repairs and Rentals

Country Pedalers Inc. offers bicycle rentals and complete bicycle repair. They are located conveniently on the shores of the Allegheny at the southern point of the Samuel Justice Trail and almost at the beginning of the Allegheny River Trail. Keep this in mind. It is the only bicycle repair shop in the area that is trail-adjacent, and the owners are very nice people. Currently, they are only open Tuesday through Saturday. You can contact them at 814-432-8055.

Franklin Museums

Debence Antique Music World
1261 Liberty Street
814-432-8350
http://www.debencemusicworld.com/

Franklin Camping

Rocky Grove V.F.D. Fairgrounds
29 Wood Street
814-432-2648

Two Mile Run
471 Beach Road
814-676-6116
http://www.twomilerun.net/

Franklin Hotel & Motels

The Idlewood Motel
1566 Mercer Road
814-437-3003
http://www.idlewoodmotel-storage.com/

Quality Inn and Conference Center
1411 Liberty Street
814-437-3031
http://www.qualityinn.com/hotel-franklin-pennsylvania

Super 8 Motel
Route 8, Franklin, PA 16323
814-432-2101
http://www.super8.com/

Franklin Bed & Breakfast

Hager's Peach Basket Bed & Breakfast

1501 Liberty Street
814-437-7699 or 800-360-6598,
http://www.hagerspeachbasket.com/

Lamberton House Bed & Breakfast
1331 Otter Street
814-432-7908

http://www.lambertonhouse.com/

Franklin Restaurants

A thorough listing of restaurants in Franklin
can be found at:
http://www.franklinpa.gov/v_restaurants.asp

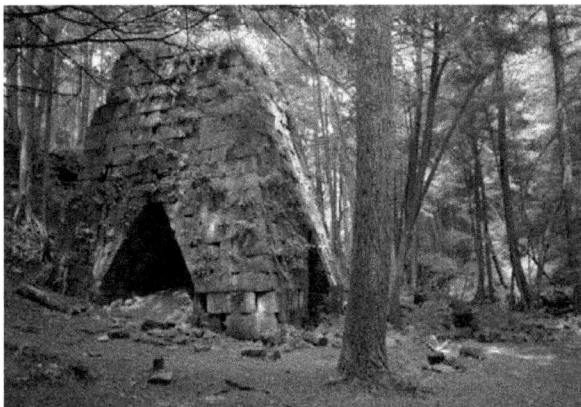

***Rockland Iron Furnace: Just one of the
many historical sites along this pristine,
remote, and vast trail system.***

The Allegheny River Trail

The Allegheny River trail begins in
Franklin. Parking for this part of the trail is
located in the south part of town. In addition
to ample parking spaces, there is an
information center, a stretching area, a boat
launch, picnic tables, and porta potties in the
summer season. There is also a bicycle shop
here if you need any repairs on your ride.

While writing this guide, every time I
rode from Franklin to Belmar, I was alone. I
do not recommend this, though, on many of
the trails because some are quite remote, and
having a buddy along just makes sense. But
this beginning portion of the trail is very well-
traveled and has many points of exit;
consequently, many people do choose to travel
it without company.

Loving the outdoors, I have ridden all the trails many times. At first, my friends wanted to go along for the adventure, but after taking them on long treks and hiking off every unpaved trail to explore, they all decided my excursions were too intense.

I have spent my entire life hiking and biking. Most people do not have this type of conditioning, though, and taking them on a long trek can turn them off on the trails, especially young children.

Although biking long distances was required for me to thoroughly prepare this guide, I do not recommend this practice for novice trail-users. And that is one of the great things about this beginning portion of the trail: the level, paved trail has several parking areas that serve as access points, so the distance one covers can easily be adjusted and there are adequate benches on which to pause and catch one's breath. The rewarding sights on these trails are not limited to pretty scenes and viewing wildlife: one always sees families enjoying activities on the trails. The outdoor environment provides a natural setting in which family members can interact and share an inexpensive and healthy outing. It is a wonderful way to bond.

Because all of the trails are handicap accessible, there are many people who are able to enjoy the trails in spite of any physical limitations. Even if one cannot pedal or ride a bike, special bicycles with hand pedals or other accommodations can insure that even people with disabilities can enjoy the wilderness by utilizing the level surfaces of the paved trails. Electric wheelchairs are also permitted on all the trails.

When I first agreed to write this guide, I realized that I would have to conquer several personal fears. I am petrified of snakes, mice, and several other creatures that I would likely encounter. And I did meet them. However, the more I went out on the trails and successfully faced these fears, the more empowered I felt. I have yet to come back from a ride without feeling proud of myself for doing just that.

There's a reason for me providing this confession: I want any reader of this trail guide to realize that any personal apprehensions you may have about using the trail can also be mastered. It's really not scary out there.

Throughout life, I have found that many city streets contain far more dangers that must be watched for and avoided. One simply has to be cautious in any environment. But to fully experience life, one has to get out there and give it a try. I suspect that you, too, will never regret moving forward. I'm sure that on each ride or hike that you take --- whether on a portion of the rail that is quite familiar or if on a new portion of the trail --- you will be rewarded with many positive experiences.

Parking Area for Allegheny River Trail in South Franklin

Mile Marker 0

Mileage Sign

Allegheny River Trail South Mile Marker 0 - .5

At mile marker 0, there is a sign that helps you estimate the mileage for your adventure. It reads: Belmar, 5.1 miles south; Brandon, 10.0 miles south; and Oil City, 5.5 miles north. You have a choice of two trails: heading south is the Allegheny River Trail while leading north is the Samuel Justice Trail. Mile marker 0 begins the Allegheny River Trail that stretches all the way to the city of Parker.

The trail begins with a steep bank off to the right toward the river. On the left, a rainbow of wildflowers greets you during most seasons. This portion of the trail is well-traveled and many use the well-worn path on the right for cross-country running.

As mentioned previously, this is a great section of the trail for beginning bikers and hikers because it offers short trip access points.

The trail is level and paved, and as you follow the trail downstream, the gradual grade is hardly noticeable. The entire trail system observes similar grades thus allowing even a novice rider or hiker to easily make the trek.

Allegheny River Trail South Mile Marker .5 – 1

Between these mile markers is the first historical plaque along the Allegheny River Trail. It describes a famous bridge --- the Big Rock Highway Toll Bridge --- that existed there until an ice jam took it out in 1926. Before then, the toll bridge had been a major thoroughfare for horses and wagons and then automobiles.

Remains of Big Rock Bridge by Plaque

In 1901, ownership of the toll bridge changed hands, and the new owners added an upper deck for street cars. As the plaque points out, the bridge got its name from the huge rock clearly visible across the river. While this boulder is particularly noteworthy for its size, many places along the Allegheny River Trail possess similar rocky cliffs and other large boulders will be seen jutting out from the river banks. As this is the very beginning of the trail, you still hear some noise from the highway as you travel southward, but the sounds of the city soon dissipate and are replaced by Nature's sounds.

There is another important and interesting plaque along this short section of the trail: it is the John Wilkes Booth plaque. Most people know that Booth was Abraham Lincoln's assassin, and some will remember that Booth was an actor by trade. What is unfamiliar to most, though, is that at one time Booth lived in Franklin, PA and ventured into his oil business. This plaque explains that tidbit of history and marks the location of his less-than-productive oil well. Students of history can only speculate about the possible impact on American history had Booth's well been a gusher and made him a rich man. The plaque provides unique photographs and additional information about John Wilkes Booth, such as that after the assassination of President Lincoln, there was a greater demand for photographs of John Wilkes Booth than of the late president, so much so that the government outlawed the buying and selling of Booth's pictures. According to the plaque, everyone in Franklin who knew Booth was surprised that the mild-mannered and good-looking man who never talked about politics had committed such a terrible deed.

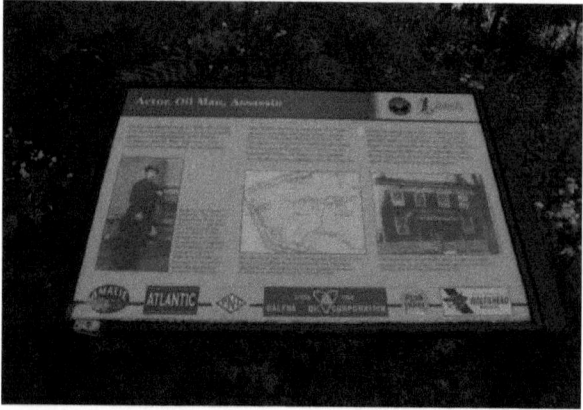

Historical Plaque on trail about John Wilkes Booth

The plaque's location just before mile marker 1 makes it an easily-accessible historical site that even young children can visit for a hands-on experience of local and American history.

Mile Marker 1

Allegheny River Trail South Mile Marker 1-1.5

As you begin this section of trail, the distance between the bank of the river and the trail increases. You might still hear a little street noise, but your attention will soon be directed to the wild lilies and the rainbow array of wildflowers that greet you along the trail.

Adorondack Camping Shelters

Just past mile marker 1, there is a camping site that is definitely "5 Stars" for this trail. The trees provide a shaded canopy and there are flat, elevated areas for off-the-ground camping. Also, two Adirondack shelters, a dozen picnic tables, and two porta-potties have been provided. There is a great view of the river here, and with no houses visible across the river, the feeling of remoteness is complete.

This is a great spot for family or group camping because it has easy access just in case of a medical emergency. It is strategically located between the Franklin parking area and the Deep Hollow parking area that is only about four-tenth of a mile to the south.

Continuing south on the trail, you will see a drainage pipe that pours water from a stream into the river. This gives you a preview of what the Allegheny River Trail offers the rider, because you will encounter a variety of waterfalls as you travel along.

In the river, you will see one of the many islands that harbor a variety of wildlife species. Several large trees dominate the center of this particular island and provide perches for birds of prey like eagles or the osprey who enjoy the abundant quantity of fish that swim in the river here.

Located near the 1.4 mile marker is the Deep Hollow Parking Area. This parking place is accessed from Route 322 by turning off at the Brine Treatment Plant south of Franklin. While this lot does not offer facilities, it is a convenient way to shorten the scenic trip to Belmar.

Immediately before arriving at the Deep Hollow Parking Area, you will come to a bridge going over Moody Run. With the rapid stream passing through old tunnels beneath and the panoramic view available from the bridge itself, pausing here for a moment provides great visual rewards.

Wooden Bridge Across Deep Hollow

Deep Hollow Parking Area

Just past the bridge is a well-walked
path that leads down to the river. There are
many good fishing spots along the river, and
the most direct path from the paved trail leads
to a campfire ring. The river bank here is lined
with huge ferns throughout summer, and the
tree branches provide a shaded cover beneath
which one can cool off on a warm day. As
there are high weeds here, wearing long pants
is advised.

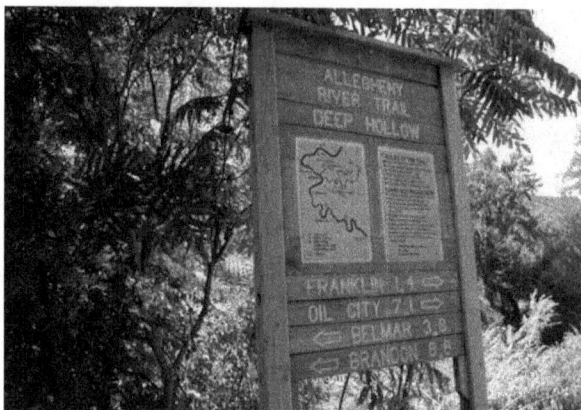

Mileage Sign at Deep Hollow Parking Area

This nice side-trail is located shortly before a sign on the trail that provides the mileage to different destinations: Franklin: 1.4 miles north; Oil City: 7.1 miles north; Belmar: 3.8 miles south; and Brandon: 8.6 miles south.

Mile Marker 1.5
Allegheny River Trail South Mile Marker 1.5-2

As you proceed south from the parking area, you pass through the common yellow gates that restrict motorized vehicles from the trail. In mid-to-late July, you will find wild raspberries on the river side of the trail, and a little further down on the left are wild blackberry bushes. Because of the abundant berries and food for birds, this entire area is a good place for avid bird watchers to "flock together." The last time I rode this trail, circling gracefully above me was a bald eagle obviously enjoying the early afternoon wind currents.

Mile Marker 2

Allegheny River Trail South Mile Marker 2-2.5

By the time you have reached mile marker 2, all the noises of the city of Franklin have disappeared leaving only the communications between the many birds, the whisper of gentle breezes, and the sounds of a flowing river. Until approaching a town, most of the Allegheny River Trail is like this stretch. The quietness of wilderness surrounds you and offers a sample of how rewarding it will be to continue proceeding further down the trail.

The smells of the city have vanished as well, replaced by the natural scents of wildflowers, the characteristic aroma of the deep woods, and the smell of the river water. Each of your senses will become attuned to Nature as you keep moving along the trail.

People have reported seeing black bears and foxes on this section of trail. They say that the baby foxes are so curious that in the spring they come right up to the edge of the trail to observe the travelers passing through. Downy woodpeckers are abundant in this area, too; it is not uncommon to hear their persistent tapping. The woods are deep here, and because water is available at the river, many game paths cut across the paved trail from the wooded areas down to the river.

Bench between mile marker 2 and 2.5

About half way between mile marker 2 and 2.5 is a bench from which one can take in a scenic overlook of the river. It provides a great view of a grassy island, one of many in the river, and a central pillar that still remains in the river from the now-long-gone Big Rock Bridge. There is no shade here, though, so using this bench as a rest stop on a hot day is not as rewarding.

The last time I rode this section of the trail, I spotted two bald eagles soaring together on the wind currents. The entire area from Oil City to Parker offers an abundance of wildlife which, surprisingly, often seems oblivious to the noises of the city, and as a result, many animals are frequently seen by people using the Allegheny River Trail.

Proceeding southward along the trail, you will soon encounter a historical plaque that provides information about the Hoover Well. According to the plaque, the Hoover Well was drilled in the 1860's and was actually only the third commercial oil well drilled in the entire world. In addition to details about the well, the plaque points out the well's precise location and contains background information explaining the historical significance of the area.

Blue Heron love this area. It is not uncommon to see one of these majestic birds fishing off the banks of the islands.

Clutter remains from the days when the Oil Boom dominated the area. An old oil pump sits off to the left just before you arrive at mile marker 2.5. Unlike some of the other pumps located along the trail that are still actively pumping oil, this relic is merely a rusty reminder of its long-ago functional days.

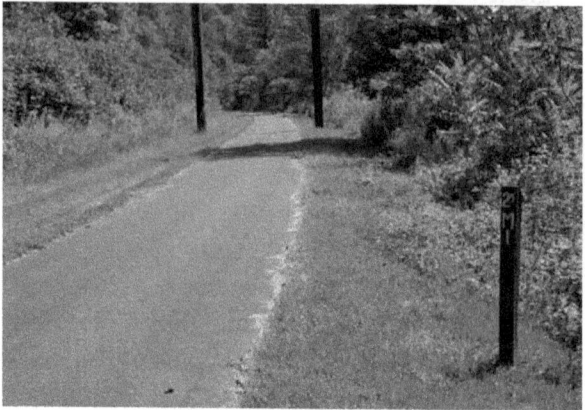

Mile Marker 2.5
Allegheny River Trail South Mile Marker 2.5 - 3

Although this area is quite remote, it is rather open and there is little shade available for relief on hot summer days. There is a bench approximately halfway between these mile markers that offers a place to rest and provides a nice view of the river.

Bench between mile marker 2.5 and 3

The paths that lead off into the woods along this stretch are generally game trails. Thus, a wide variety of wildlife can often be seen along here.

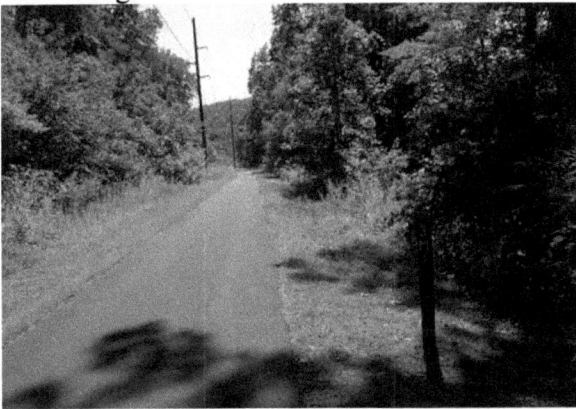

Mile Marker 3

Allegheny River Trail South Mile Marker 3 - 3.5

This is a nice section of the trail because it offers a glimpse of the remoteness you will find further down river, and, paradoxically, because of the power lines that run along it. As evidenced by the large quantity of droppings beneath the power lines, many birds take advantage of the wires as a place to perch; often birds of prey will balance there while surveying the area for a meal.

Looking across the river, one can see the stately mansions that were built years ago; apparently enjoying the magnificent view of the mighty Allegheny River is a timeless endeavor. Recalling an even earlier era in history, it is difficult to juxtapose the humble villages of the Native Americans who almost certainly once lived here.

Continuing, huge boulders start to line the left side of the trail. Northwestern Pennsylvania's natural resources are not limited to oil and gas; reportedly many immense stones were transported down river and used to construct many of the buildings that still stand in Pittsburgh today.

Mile Marker 3.5

Proceeding through this section, you will hear various sounds of the wilderness that this remote area of the Allegheny River Trail offers. Additionally, the sounds of the river water passing over and between the large boulders contribute to the audible treat.

Another island begins to form in the river at this point, and approximately halfway between these mile markers is a bench from which one can relax and enjoy the view. If fortunate, one may catch a glimpse of the wildlife that lives on these small islands.

Bench between Mile Marker 3.5 and 4

A little further south, there is a steep trail that leads down to the river. Once there, you'll find a flat spot that could easily be utilized for camping, but, being quite rustic, there is no fire ring. A more conventional camping spot is located only 300 yards downstream where metal stairs gradually lead

51

one down to a nice, grassy area. It is a well-maintained area and has two picnic tables and a firering

Camping Area between Mile Marker 3.5 and 4

Many game trails lead from the dense woods on the left of the trail as you proceed. This is indicative of the vast number of animals you might encounter in the area.

Mile Marker 4

Allegheny River Trail South Mile Marker 4 - 4.5

Because this stretch of trail is very remote, you will see many different wild animals, or at least evidence they've been there. Traveling early in the morning and late in the evening, as previously mentioned, greatly increases the likelihood of seeing wildlife. Birdwatchers will particularly enjoy the amazing number of birds like cardinals and indigo buntings who have been attracted to the area.

Just past where the sound of water flowing into the river greets you is a trail off to the right that leads down to the river. It is a great rustic camping spot because it has a fire ring, and a stream enhances the soothing sounds of flowing water.

There are two trees here that every trail user or guide reader should try to see. These two trees represent some of the very few old-growth trees that are still in existence in our region. These two were never harvested for lumber, ironically, because their deformities caused them to be passed-over by loggers for better specimens. One of these trees is completely hollow in the center; it would provide decent shelter if needed during a sudden rain storm. These old-growth trees allow us to witness a glimpse of what "Penn's Woods" originally looked like when Native Americans lived here and before the Europeans arrived with their determination to clear-cut forests in the name of progress.

A red-tailed hawk's nest is located shortly before you reach mile marker 4.5. The screams that fill the afternoon air might startle you as you travel on the trail. Sharing the parenting duties, both the male and female red-tailed hawks tend to the nest and the fledglings. Consequently, both "mom" and "dad" may dive at you should they determine that you are too close to their nest. Their protective instincts could pose dangers to the unsuspecting human traveler.

Mile Marker 4.5

Allegheny River Trail South Mile Marker 4.5 - 5

From this part of the trail, looking toward the rocky shore of the island, you may see turtles basking in the sun. There are many varieties of turtles that live along the river.

Just before you reach mile marker 5, on the left you'll see a large, old, wooden water tank. Tanks such as these served an important function for the railroads as they stored water used to replenish the steam engines. These trains not only allowed commerce to boom throughout the oil region but provided vital transportation links for people as well. A tank such as this is an important reminder of the crucial role that the railroads, whose rails have been removed and their track beds transformed into the trails we now enjoy, once performed.

From here, the Belmar Bridge can be seen to the south, and signs of civilization are once again visible across the river.

Mile Marker 5

Allegheny River Trail South Mile Marker 5 - 5.5

Just beyond mile marker 5 is a bench that provides a resting point from which to look at the river and the north side of the Belmar Bridge. Because Belmar is a small town with few inhabitants, this remains a remote and quiet point on the trail. Actually, most of the river villages provide similar serenity.

Bench between Mile Marker 5 and 5.6

This section of the trail is particularly good for bird watching. In my adventures along here, I've spotted a wide variety of birds during each season. The area attracts birds because it is rich with berries, bugs, and dense foliage. Almost as if it were a terminal at a busy airport, during the spring and fall this area is visited by a variety of waterfowl and other birds on their way to distant destinations. Thus, this is an excellent place from which to catch a glimpse of birds that are not indigenous to western Pennsylvania.

Trail between Mile Marker 5.0 and 5.6

Proceeding southward, the paved trail leads you through an old steel railroad barrier. Beside the pavement is a wooden walkway, but it is not very level. Wild blackberries and grapes climb the steel walls of this old railroad barrier and provide a tasty treat for all kinds of creatures who savor these delights.

At this point, Belmar Bridge towers over you. There is a mowed pathway off to the left. This, although it is not markered as such, is a private driveway. Many of the mowed trails leading off the bike path are designated for the users of the trail. But a few are private property and should not be trespassed.

Mileage Sign at Sandy Creek Trail Intersection

Sandy Creek Trail Intersection

Immediately after the Belmar Bridge underpass, there is a plaque describing this amazing feat of engineering. This is also where one can intersect the Sandy Creek Trail and the North Country Trail.

Going southward on the left is a picnic table and a sign the indicates the direction to ascend up to the Sandy Creek Trail and the Belmar Bridge. There are steps up, but a dirt path along the side enables easy access for transporting a bicycle up to the adjoining trails.

It is well worth making this trek up to the bridge. The wildlife viewing from this vista is incredible. I saw many eagles from this vantage point on my excursions.

Mile Marker 5.5

Allegheny River Trail South Mile Marker 5.5 - 6

Just past mile marker 5.5 is a bench that provides a nice place from which to take in the picturesque view of the south side of the Belmar Bridge. Blackberries are in abundance here in July. Like the previous bench, it is a great place to relax while watching birds.

View of Belmar Bridge from bench between mile marker 5.5 and 6

This stretch of trail is open; there are few trees with overhanging limbs to provide shade. There is a trail off to the left that is steep and dangerous, although temptingly, it leads to an old stone water bowl that once was used to supply water for steam engines. Off to the left, there is a waterfall, but generally it is visible only in the spring and fall because lush vegetation tends to hide it during the summer.

Mile Marker 6.0 South

Allegheny River Trail South Mile Marker 6 - 6.5

Visually enhancing one's journey along this area of the trail is an abundance of wildflowers. In front of you, the view of the river expands to a beautiful panoramic scene. The houses across the river slowly fade away as you proceed and are replaced by the uncluttered natural environment. Continuing a little further, a waterfall once again gives you a hint of what is to come. As you will see, proceeding forward there are many waterfalls situated along the next thirty miles of trails.

Campsite between mile marker 6 and 6.5

As you go further south, cattails line the left of the trail, and then you will find a mowed area off to the right. Beautiful ferns blanket the river bank in front of a campsite. This is a nice camping area with two picnic tables, a bench, and a designated fire ring. It is a very well kept area, and because it is close enough to Belmar should an emergency occur, it provides both a beautiful and quite safe location for families or groups to camp.

Mile marker 6.5

Allegheny River Trail South Mile Marker 6.5 - 7

Situated between these two distance markers is another wooden water tank, one of many relics from the days when railroads were the dominant means of transportation and oil was the king of commerce. Viewing these remaining relics reminds one of the historical significance of this region through which the Allegheny Valley Trails System passes.

Shortly beyond the water tank is a waterfall on the left, but it only flows after a heavy rain or after the warm days of spring have melted away winter's snow. On the left, a small stream begins accompanying the trail. The last time I passed through here, I heard the sound of a baby fox calling. Many people have reported seeing these inquisitive young pups either directly on or just off the side of the trail watching as bike riders pedal by.

During July, the vixen (mother fox) forces the pups to leave the den to survive independently on their own. Fox are meat-eaters who feed on small rodents, rabbits, and even carrion. At risk of being redundant, I will once again remind readers that they should never try to pet one of these animals. Although they may look adorable, they are wild creatures, and, especially if they feel threatened, they may bite you.

A little further down the trail is a waterfall edged by cattails. The rock has a distinctive reddish-orange hue caused by iron in the water. These rich iron deposits brought wealth to the region long before the oil boom. Back in the 1700's, people built huge iron furnaces to produce pig iron. As later would be the case with successful oil wells, entire communities developed around these furnaces which produced such a much-in-demand product.

Seen lining the steep walls to the south is slate rock, another indication of the area's richness in natural resources. Be careful of the bank's sharp drop-off to the river.

Continuing, soon you will be greeted by two more waterfalls. Although they gush water only in the spring and just after heavy rainstorms, one does seem to drip constantly. These are just a tease; be forewarned that some of the waterfalls yet to come will take your breath away.

Just before mile marker 7 are steps that lead down to a platform overlooking the river. This is private property. It is important that all trail-users respect and avoid areas like this. Occasionally the trail passes directly through a private individual's land, and the trail exists only because the landowner has graciously granted permission to the trail association. Thus, all trail users should be mindful and appreciative of the landowner for granting passage.

Mile marker 7.0

Allegheny River Trail South Mile Marker 7.0 - 7.5

Just past mile marker 7, on the river side is a trail, but it is actually a game trail blazed by animals. It is very steep, and I advise that you do not follow this path because you will soon come to many better points from which to access the river.

During spring and early summer, vibrant yellow wildflowers line the next section of trail. Another waterfall is located here, but you will most likely only hear it and not see it because during most of the year, leaf-laden branches hide the waterfall from view.

Mile marker 7.5

Allegheny River Trail South Mile Marker 7.5 - 8

Ferns and cattails cover most of the left bank along this portion of the trail, and the power lines that have stretched along the trail soon disappear. At this point, you realize that mostly wilderness stretches ahead. The trees provide a welcome canopy here, making it a particularly pleasant area for a cool and shady ride or walk.

Looking to the river, one will notice a grassy island surfacing from the river's depths while on bank near where the railroad's rails once ran is another wooden water tank.

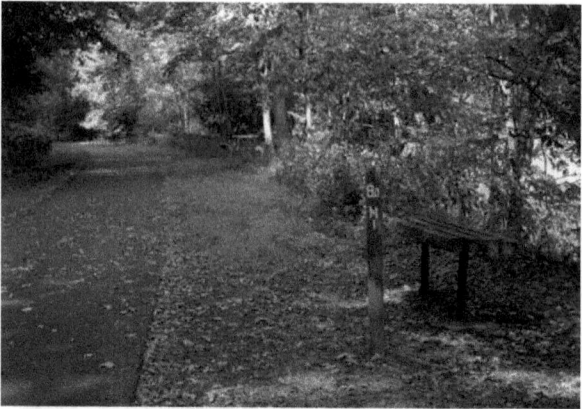

Mile Marker 8.0

Allegheny River Trail South Mile Marker 8 - 8.5

Just past mile marker 8 is a bench with a nice view of the river, and approximately 30 feet beyond that is a picnic table. As trees provide shade, the table is a great place at which to stop and soak in the remoteness of the area.

Proceeding further southward, the scent of blooming mountain laurel greets you in spring, and blooming rhododendron bushes delight the trail user in early summer. As both are evergreen bushes, they provide year-round greenery for trail-users.

There is a dripping (in summer) waterfall on the left as you proceed, and on the left a bit further down are two oil storage tanks. One is steel and one is plastic, this illustrates that the area is still rich with oil. Many of the oil wells that were drilled back in the oil boom era are still pumping oil today.

Wooden platform that overlooks Indian God Rock

Continuing southward is Indian God Rock. For me, Indian God Rock is one of the most spiritual places along the Allegheny Valley Trail Association's many trails. I invite you to pause for a moment here and see if you, too, feel the beauty of the area fill you with a sense of mysticism. Sometimes when I am here, quietly reflecting, I have seen a beaver or two moving around on the rocks below.

Beaver gathering food at Indian God Rock

Petroglyphs at Indian God Rock

Scores of decades ago, Native Americans carved petroglyphs --- carvings of spiritual animals --- on these rocks. Legend suggests that this site was used by a shaman (Native American medicine man) to communicate with the spirits and also as a place in which to teach Indian children.

The plaque that marks this sacred spot is very informative; it highlights the history of the site and states, "The petroglyphs on the Indian God Rock are among the earliest noted by Europeans in the Upper Ohio Valley."

It also supplies additional details about the Native Americans who once inhabited the area. It states that between 1200 and 1750, Native Americans who lived here spoke the Algonquian language. The plaque also displays a very early picture of Indian God Rock when the petroglyphs from these people were much easier to see.

In addition to the information about Native Americans, the plaque explains that it was French explorer Pierre Joseph Celeron de Banville who in 1749 performed the task of burying lead plates in the area in order to claim the surrounding territory for France.

Since the early European travelers first come to the river, they have been drawn to visit this location. Unfortunately the white man's markings now prevail, and the original petroglyphs on this rock are barely visible. People who probably would have never considered leaving graffiti along the walls of a church or temple, had no qualms about similarly desecrating this sacred spot, and, sadly, have selfishly marred the site.

***Steep path leading down to Indian God Rock
lined with poison ivy***

Along here is a wonderful wooden
deck with a railing that makes a great
observation point, or, since there are also
benches, it is a convenient place to take a
break and perhaps embrace the spirituality of
the trail. The trail that leads from the deck
down to the rock is covered with poison ivy,
and I do not recommend that you travel down

it. Even if you manage to avoid the poison ivy, the path itself is extremely steep and dangerous. If you would become injured, it would take a long time to obtain help.

However, be sure to look to the water to see if you can catch a glimpse of the beavers who live here. Their den appears to be in the rocks, and particularly in the early mornings or evenings, you can often see them busy at work or play.

Sunrise at Indian God Rock

Spirituality surrounds The Allegheny Valley River Trail. One spot attracts me to it the most though, and that is Indian God Rock. Most of the petroglyphs that marked the spot with a special mythical language conveyed through carvings of animals disappeared with the constant rising and falling of the might river's early-uncontained ebb and flow. Since the early discovery of this spot by settlers, it also became desiccated by people who seemed to need to mark their presence. In my eyes, they are like the people that enjoy knocking over gravestones or destroying holy statues in front of a church that stood there for decades looking out unscathed by human touch.

By writing about this holy place, I know it will become very popular, and that I am giving away an amazing secret to the trail. I am begging my readers to please not leave their mark on this sacred Native American landmark. If you stand quiet at this spot for any length of time, you will realize that God already knows you were there. Maybe that is why the early settlers named this Indian God Rock.

I will never grow tired of visiting this sacred site. It calls to me and tells me that if I visit, I will find answers and riches. I find both on every occasion.

One day, I felt that calling so deeply that I knew I had to listen to it. I decided then that experiencing a sunrise there would once again provide me with the answers my soul required and an experience that I would never forget in my lifetime. I received both and much more that cool summer morning. I only have my camera, these words and God to mark my time on the spot; all are more than enough of a reward.

I awoke at 4 A.M that morning. As I pried myself out the door, it reminded me of the two and a half years that I delivered newspapers. I reveled in the early hours in my youth. That morning, I questioned my sanity in those younger years.

Dressed in sweats to fend off the damp coldness of the morning on the river, I headed out on the drive up river to the Brandon Parking area. The drive alone was reward enough for the morning, and as I progressed, I knew I was doing the right thing at the right time.

First, a doe and two fawns crossed in front of me. Then two bucks with fresh velvet darted over a steep embankment heading down to the sleepy village. Within seconds, I spotted two doe. With these visual rewards even before I headed out on the trail, there was no doubt in my mind the morning would hold many delights.

When I parked, there were no sounds in the village besides the first birds calling to the sunrise. Because it was colder outside than the river temperature, thick fog enveloped the entire area. There was no gorgeous river view at that point. The dense clouds of fog erased the normal visual rewards as I headed down the trail.

As my blood started pumping with the ride, the damp air started penetrating my clothing. Right about the time, I determined that I was insane for venturing out that early on such a cold morning, I arrived at Indian God Rock.

I parked my bike off the trail, and as I proceeded down the perilous incline, the insanity thought once again crossed my mind. I knew heading down the torturous slope that if I hurt myself, no one would find me for quite some time. I was on my own with the poison ivy; the decent, the rapid river, and the huge boulders that beckoned me sit upon them.

To my delight, I made it safely to a rock next to Indian God Rock, where I chose to settle. The Allegheny River is narrow there, and I decided it would give my lens the perfect vantage point to capture any wildlife that ventured through the thick haze.

At that point, the fog was still so dense that I could not see the other side of the river. I could only see clearly about thirty feet in front of me. Once again, I asked myself if I was crazy. Within seconds, I saw a log or something in front of me. As my eyes focused in, I could not get my camera in front of my face fast enough. It was a beaver carrying saplings within feet of me. As I snapped away capturing the moment, it submersed near by me under a rock. I surmised immediately that I was almost sitting upon its den. What a blessing! Because they are mostly nocturnal animals, I felt like I was presented a huge gift to see it carrying its midnight snack to bed. I usually only see them late in the evenings.

By this time, I was no longer questioning the method to my madness. I could not keep my eyes off the ever-changing scene on the river. The variable contrasts and hues as the first of the suns beams ate their way through the dense fog mesmerized my camera and me. I clicked away hopping from boulder to boulder attempting to capture every magical moment.

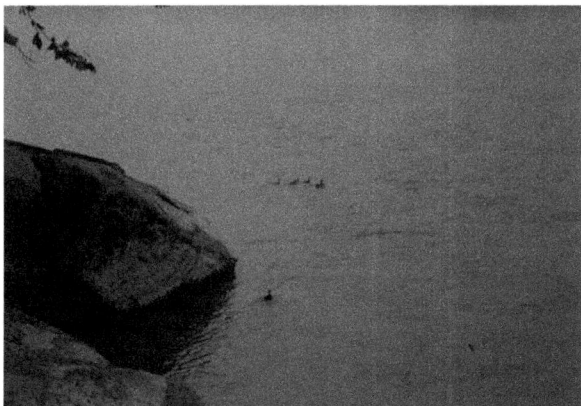

Gander and baby ducks stirred up at sunrise

My traversing stirred a gander and some baby ducks from their safe nesting place, and I decided that I had better settle in fear that I might disturb something else that still needed a few more winks. Steam rolled off the river in layers at different times in front of my eyes.

Great Blue Heron at sunrise

I could almost focus on the distant shoreline when a great blue heron flew into my viewfinder. Grateful that I had fast shutter speed, I clicked away and once again captured a priceless moment in time.

Great Blue Heron in flight

The great blue heron is the largest of all herons. They are a common sight upon the Allegheny River, because the grassy islands and shorelines provide an abundant feeding ground for them to spear their next victim with their sharp bills. Their keen senses allow them to feed early in the morning hours and late into the evenings. Spotting a great blue heron on the river is not rare, but experiencing the moment as they maneuver their great wingspan over a foggy river is surreal.

By the time the sun's rays devoured the last bits of steam and fog that blanketed the river, the cold began penetrating my clothing enough to cause uncontrolled shivering. I reprimanded myself for not dressing more appropriately and not being prepared for anything as I climbed my way back up the steep slippery incline.

As I maneuvered my bike towards a break in the dense canopy blocking the sun, forced from the spiritual spot by the elements, I recanted all my trepidations as I set out earlier that morning. I rebuked each one as the feeling became present in my hands. That cold early morning, like every other time I visited that amazingly spiritual place, was one that burns in my memory. Although my body still shivered from the damp cold, my soul felt complete. I felt richer than anyone alive at that moment, and I continued down my path in life towards my next adventure on the trail.

. . .

Old wooden water tank left from the days when steam locomotion still operated in the area

A little ways down the trail is another old wooden water tank leftover from the steam engine era. The last time I paused here taking notes, I spotted a small fawn watching me from the woods. There are many white-tailed deer here, and seeing them is very common. Because the trail does not permit motorized vehicles, the wildlife often seem to accept passers-by with curiosity rather than perceiving us as threats.

Moving south toward the next mile marker, as the sounds of the wilderness dominate, you will continue coming across silent reminders that reflect the historic past of the oil boom era including an old, rusty pipeline that runs parallel to the trail and another wooden water tank.

Mile marker 9.0

Allegheny River Trail South Mile Marker 9.0 - 10

Continuing southward, ferns line the tree-covered trail, and on the river side the bank drops off to a grassy flatland.

Off 322, Astral Road Parking Lot, another waterfall greets you to the left, and emptying into the river, it creates a pretty scene. Another photo-worthy sight can be seen from the bench where one views an old railroad bridge crossing the river as the Sandy Creek Trail leads to Fisherman's Cove.

View of bridge over Big Sandy Creek from bench

Not much further down on the right is a great shady picnic table that invites you to dine outdoors. There is a waterfall on the left that runs fluidly and can be seen from the trail.

Picnic area between mile marker 9.5 and 10

At this point, as indicated by the yellow trail gate, you are entering the village of Brandon. The paths, however, that lead to the river and the one on the left are both private property and should not be followed.

Just before you arrive at mile marker 10 there is a sign stating the mileage to various destinations: Belmar, 4.8 miles north; Franklin, 10 miles north; and Oil City, 15.7 miles north. This sign provides an opportunity for a unique photograph because just above the writing, there are two spaces in which you can place your face in the sign.

Brandon Acres Snack Shop

Allegheny River Trail South Mile Marker 10-11

Proceeding southward from mile marker 10, the signs of civilization once again begin to appear. Private property signs line both sides of the trail. Not far into this little town of Brandon, you will see a playground set and a wooden building on the left. This is Brandon Acres Snack Shop. It is a self-serve shop that allows you to purchase water, snacks, and other items on a trust basis. This is a great place to restock on water or purchase some quick chocolate for energy on the trail.

A place to purchase these necessities is needed here on this trail. It is a great thing that the owners did to establish this facility. Please be respectful and honest when visiting this establishment.

Brandon Parking Area

Not too much further is the Brandon Parking Area. It has ample parking, but it is a little rough at the end of the road before you get to the parking area.

The next 4.5 miles of this stretch has no public benches or picnic tables. If you want to rest, Brandon Acres is a nice place to stop.

As you proceed southward from the Brandon Parking Area, the trail leads you through the small quiet town of Brandon. A private dirt road runs along side the bike trail through this section allowing private landowners to access their property. The speed limit is only 10 miles an hour through this section, so the very few cars that you may meet present no worries.

The trail winds southward through this pretty village, and green lawns that surround well-kept houses greet you through this entire area. Across the river, you will see the small village of Fisherman's Cove, and not too much further after the Brandon Parking Area, you will see a sign on the west side of the trail that says 113 in big letters. This is not an address for the home across the street. It is a mile marker that indicates the number of miles to Pittsburgh following the railroad tracks going southward. Along the Allegheny River Trail, you will see many of these signs. As highway markers today provide the same type of information for motorists, these signs would tell the train engineers their exact location and how far they still had to travel.

Mile Marker 11.0 South

Allegheny River Trail South Mile Marker
11-11.5

As the river starts to twist westward, the trail winds with it through the rest of the small village and its summer cottages. By the time you reach mile marker 11, you are almost out of the town.

Several streams feed into the river through this stretch, and wildlife is abundant regardless of the human habitation. Birds of prey such as red-tailed hawks and eagles thrive throughout this part of the trail. Most of the homes are only occupied in the summer; the quiet tranquility that these landowners embrace makes it a welcoming home for a variety of wildlife.

Just before mile marker 11.5, a small island appears in the river. Like the many small islands that emerge from the constant flowing water of the Allegheny River, this little island is a haven for blue heron and other waterfowl. It provides a shallow shore for fishing and an uninterrupted nesting place in spring for further propagation.

Mile Marker 11.5 South

Allegheny River Trail South Mile Marker 11.5-12

Mile Marker 11.5 is the last mile marker as you leave Brandon. Within 50 yards of this mile marker, yellow barriers once again appear restricting access to any motorized vehicle traffic.

I traveled through this area in mid-March and spotted two eagles high in the sky diving at each other. It was extraordinary behavior because it is indicative of how they breed and usually eagles breed in January and February. By mid-March, eagles are usually protectively sitting on their eggs and sharing turns to hunt. When one parent leaves the nest, the other gently takes over keeping the egg warm. Like many birds, both the male and female eagles tend to their offspring. Male and female eagles both have white heads and tails and look very similar. Many male birds of other species are more colorful than female counterparts, and many do not participate in helping raise the young. For example, male songbirds are generally much more colorful than the females, and the male songbirds usually do not share in the raising of the young. When the males and females have hardly any color difference, it is usually indicative that they share task of providing for the young.

Eagles are known as thieves and will often dive and fight for food even from each other. But when they are high in the sky, this is not a common behavior unless they are breeding. One can only assume from the spectacle I observed that day in March that these two eagles found each other rather late.

Continuing southward, huge boulders covered with bright green moss can be seen along the east side of the trail. Off to the right, there is a trail down to the river. A sign markered here states that there is no overnight camping without written permission. It is clearly private property, but the landowner is gracious enough to not marker any "No Trespassing" signs. This is a nice spot to rest and take in the sights that constantly appear on the river. There is no campfire ring here, but there is a huge rock that is on the river, and it is easily accessed at this point.

Through the entire following section all the way to the Kennerdell Tunnel, Clear Creek State Forest lies directly across the river. At one time, almost all the trees around here were harvested for building or to fuel the iron furnaces that littered this iron-rich area. Now, the second-growth trees along here are huge and stand proud offering a haven for birds of prey.

On the eastern side of the trail, hemlocks --- the Pennsylvania state tree --- and hardwoods intermingle along the steep rocky banks. This is a quiet and scenic stretch of trail. Eagles are abundant throughout this section; watch the tree line across the river, and you are almost guaranteed to spot an eagle enjoying the wind currents while soaring high above the dense woodlands.

A white plastic pipe pokes out from the hillside and acts as a conduit for a spring here. This a good place to water your horses or gather camp water. If you want to drink it yourself, though, I highly recommend using purification tablets.

One of the things that I loved about this section of the trail was the number of woodpeckers that inhabit this woodland. Each time I rode through this part, the sights and sounds of the pilated woodpecker enhanced my ride.

The bank to the west of the trail drops steeply to the river through here, and there is no river access, but the eastern bank with its rocky ledges and evergreen hemlocks offers beauty in all seasons.

Before you get to mile marker 12, another small tributary feeds the mighty Allegheny River. This area is wealthy with springs, and each one adds music to the trip by offering the magical sounds of trickling water.

Mile Marker 12.0 South

Allegheny River Trail Mile Marker 12-12.5

This section of trail is another piece of priceless wonder along the river trail. It is remote, and huge rocky cliffs harbor hemlocks and hardwoods. Hemlock trees require shade to grow; without the maples, oaks and other hardwood trees to shelter them, the hemlocks could not grow or recover. The ample springs through this section are also necessary for the hemlocks.

Across the river in Clear Creek State Forest, you will also sporadically spot huge sycamore trees. They are easily recognized by their white bark, and many birds love to nest in this type of tree. Eagle and osprey particularly like these trees because sycamores often line the banks of the river or large streams, and from the branches of these tall trees, the birds enjoy a bird's eye view of what lies below in the river.

This area is especially attractive in the spring and after a good rainfall because the steep, rocky shale banks on the eastern side of the trail often become transformed into beautiful little waterfalls. Listen and look for woodpeckers through here, too. Almost every time I have passed through here, I spotted some.

Going southward, the trail winds to the west following the snake-like course of the river, and soon Withrop Island comes into view. The river side of the trail is steep, but on the eastern side of the trail, the mountainside slowly becomes less steep. The trees are still large, and the woods are uninhabited through this section. The last time I ventured down this section, I heard an eagle screeching. Because it was in March, I assumed it was a male or female impatiently calling its mate back to the nest for its shift with the eggs.

Right before mile marker 12.5, you begin to enter the small village of Sunny Slopes. After the late 1800's, this area was almost completely uninhabited. But in 1973, Otto Schiberl Sr. was fishing in the area, and along the river, he found an overgrown cabin. He immediately fell in love with it. He bought the little place and helped maintain the rocky dirt road that is the only route in and out of the tiny village. After his discovery and purchase of the cabin, the area began drawing people and developed into the growing village you see today.

Mile Marker 12.5

Allegheny River Trail South Mile Marker
12.5-13.5

Right after mile marker 12.5, the bike trail veers to the left and abandons the path of the old railroad bed. Instead, the trail follows a small road that leads through Sunny Slopes.

Through here, the trail is blazed with the blue markers of the North Country Trail and is easily followed. Right at this split-off from the trail are blackberry bushes that in season are abundant with fruit. As you proceed, Kent Road is not level, but the small hills that you traverse do not require an advanced level of riding skills.

The trail becomes paved again right before mile marker 13.5, and the gorgeous wooden fence that surrounds a trailer tells the story of why the trail in this section did not continue along the railroad bed.

Mile Marker 13.5 South

Allegheny River Trail South Mile Marker 13.5-14

Immediately after mile marker 13.5, the trail once again leads you through an isolated area. Disrupting the river's flow, huge boulders create a riffling sound.

Across the river, the woodlands of Clear Creek State Forest continue to provide spectacular scenes. Wildlife is abundant. Look to the river; wide varieties of waterfowl enjoy nesting along the shores, and eagles, red-tailed hawks, and great blue heron enjoy the unpopulated section that lies here.

As you continue southward, a clear-cut section for power lines emerges directly in front of you. This indicates where the Kennerdell Tunnel cuts through the hillside. The tunnel shaved miles off the journey to Pittsburgh by significantly reducing the distance of continuing along the river's edge.

Yellow barriers that restrict the trail from motorized vehicles once again come into view as houses again begin appearing. This is the northern part of Kennerdell. There is no public parking in Kennerdell to access the trail. Immediately before the yellow barriers, be sure to look to the eastern side of the trail; there is a rock outcropping that is obviously a den for wildlife.

Mile Marker 14.0 South

Allegheny River Trail South Mile Marker 14-14.5

Within 200 yards of mile marker 14 is the Kennerdell Tunnel. Before you get to this point though, a four-wheeler trail leads off to the east of the trail. If you need to rest before going through the tunnel, this is a nice spot to do so. The four-wheeler trail leads to a stream and is a pleasant path to hike.

The tunnel is extremely long and very dark. Once you are inside, you cannot see. I strongly recommend having a flashlight with you to illuminate your way as you pass through the tunnel. I also advise you to walk and not ride your bike through it. Because of the tunnel's immense darkness, it is easy to lose your balance when riding inside.

Northern Entrance to Kennerdell Tunnel

Spillway and Old RR Bridge before Northern Entrance to Kennerdell Tunnel

After many adventures riding the Allegheny Valley Rails to Trails, I developed a special fondness for this section of the vast trail system. Perhaps in part it is because it was the first trail that I rode after accepting the offer to write the guide. It seemed like such a daunting task and a bit overwhelming. Even after agreeing to develop a thorough guidebook, I still was not confident that I could complete it. Many miles of wilderness stretched out before me.

I owe this guide greatly in part to Dakota, my great nephew that stayed with me the summer I began riding the trails. This was the first trail we rode, and every time that I ride it now, I remember how much I enjoyed sharing the adventure with him. That first ride with Dakota gave me the courage and confidence to face every trail and complete this guide.

This particular stretch of trail winds the rider through very remote areas of wilderness, and in addition, this part of the river is designated by Congress as a wild and scenic river area. It is no wonder. The wildlife you can see on this trail is amazing. Some parts are so remote that the wildlife seems indifferent to spotting a weird looking mammal on two rubber wheels.

Kennerdell Tunnel Southern Entrance

Allegheny River Trail South Mile Marker 14.5

The south end of the Kennerdell tunnel is at approximately the 14.5-mile marker . It is an extremely long tunnel at 3350 feet, and it requires a flashlight to pass through it safely. Built in 1913, it was a great engineering feat in its day. A plaque explains in detail of what difficult task it was here at the south end of the tunnel.

Along with the informative plaque describing the tunnels creation, this spot also boasts a beautiful waterfall that flows throughout the year. It is especially exceptional though in spring when the water tables are high and the area is blessed with the showers that accompany spring and early summer.

Every time I reach this spot, I remember the first time that Dakota and I came south through this area. By this time, we already rode quite a few times, and I taught him that if we were quiet, we would see a lot of wildlife. He is very intelligent and began giving me signs instead of speaking as we rode. As we came out of the tunnel this time though, he spoke aloud, "Aunt Cindy", and pointed to the sky. There was a bald eagle souring above us greeting us as our eyes adjusted to the daylight. It was a moment in time that I hope I never forget.

The Allegheny River hosts many bald eagles and spotting them is not rare, but it always a blessing. That moment showed me that I taught Dakota a lot in our short time together. He knew to be aware of everything around him in the wilderness and never to forget to look up, or you might miss something.

It was not his first eagle sighting, but it showed me that he felt just as blessed as I did when I spotted one. Having lived on the Allegheny for years, I still remember when an eagle spotting was very rare. Now, they are flourishing throughout this clean watershed. They can even be spotted in the major towns along the trail, and more eagles seem to appear each year.

Many birds of prey like eagles, osprey, huge varieties of hawks, and occasionally peregrine falcons have chosen this vast beautiful river area for their nesting spots. The best way to know when a bird of prey is around is to listen to the crows. If the crows are squawking, there is probably a bird of prey nearby. This is when you want to look to the sky.

Birds of prey love to soar and enjoy their freedom in the sky riding the various wind currents that pass through the deep Allegheny Valley. The wind is also an indication of when to look for eagles and other birds of prey. A day on the Allegheny River hosts many changes in weather. Weather changes bring changes in wind speed, and the breeze is what these creatures love. You can sit in a spot on a windless day for hours and see nothing, but when the wind kicks up, as it does almost every day, the birds of prey take flight. The only exception to this is an extremely windy day. Paying attention to the wind changes is very rewarding. Look up!

Allegheny River Trail South Mile Marker 15-15.5

There is a picnic table and nice shady river view between these mile markers. It is a gorgeous and remote stretch of trail, and offers many visual rewards to the silent rider. The wildlife is abundant and signs of civilization are few.

Mile Marker 15.5 South

Allegheny River Trail South Mile Marker 15.5-16

Just past mile marker 15.5, you will see the remnants of an old railroad car on the left. It is one of the many signs of the vast changes the oil boom brought to the area and left behind marking the historical significance of this amazing trail system.

Old Railroad Car along the trail

You will also find a little waterfall between these mile markers on your left hand side heading south. It is one of many you will find on this stretch of the trail. I spotted an eagle here the last day I rode this trail before writing this part of the guide.

This trail, like all the Allegheny Valley Rails to Trails, rewards you for venturing off the beaten path. Right after mile marker 15.5, you will see what looks like a four-wheeler trail off to the left. I do not usually recommend following all four-wheeler trails off the paved bicycle path, but this particular trail offers a great reward.

It traverses up the side of a stream that hosts huge boulders and a great swimming hole for locals. When I went up this trail to check it out, I found a man with his two sons cooling off from the heat of the first day of summer. If it were not for them, I probably would not have gone on a four-wheeler path off the trail.

I stopped to jot down some notes on this section, when I heard loud laughter coming from the woods off to my left. This is when I spotted the four-wheeler trail and decided I needed to check it out. They were having way too much fun not to be curious, so I headed down the rugged path, watching every step along the way for snakes, poison ivy, and poison oak. It is important to watch every step you make when you are off the trail anywhere. This system of trails wanders through vast wilderness areas that can be dangerous to the novice hiker.

I am glad I took the chance that day and followed the sounds of elation. This is a great place to cool off if you want to venture off the trail and go for a swim in the cool waters that shed into the mighty Allegheny River.

After interrupting their fun by my presence, I apologized and explained that I was writing this guide. I asked the man what the name of the place was. He answered, "It's called, keep it to yourself."

We both knew at that point that I could and would not keep such a beautiful discovery from my readers. I will ask you to be respectful of other people's privacy though, and please keep this area as pristine as it was that day. If we do that, many people will laugh with elation and enjoy this piece of Mecca for years to come.

There is a beautiful area off to the left between these mile markers too. It is a deep valley filled with huge lush ferns and high grass. Large spots of crushed grass here are indicative to deer bedding down.

Mile Marker 16.0 South

Allegheny River Trail South Mile Marker 16-16.5

Vast boulders line this stretch of the Allegheny River as they do in many parts of the trail. They reveal a story of the past too. Before they erected Kinzua Dam, further north on the river, the Allegheny River would flood to great heights. Early pioneers utilized this flooding by embracing the high flow of the spring flooding to float goods down river to other communities. Many barrels of oil floated down with the high spring currents before the railroad came through to transport the black gold.

Adirondack camping shelter provided by Allegheny Valley Trail Association

If you need shelter from the weather or want an extremely nice place to camp, the Allegheny Valley Trail Association erected a great Adirondack shelter between these mile markers off to the right. There is a well-worn trail down to the shelter, but in late summer, it is hard to see the building from the trail.

It offers a covered sleeping quarter that could squeeze four people in a pinch. In addition, it has a picnic table and fire ring for overnight camping. From the river or the bike trail, this is a great camping spot and five stars for this section of the river trail. With a tremendous view of the river, you cannot ask for much more in such a remote area.

Mile Marker 16.5 South

Allegheny River Trail South Mile Marker 16.5-17

The last time that I rode this section of trail, I stopped at mile marker 16.5 to write down some notes. As I stood there writing, a deer stood less than 20 feet away from me grazing indifferent to my pen strokes and my stinky human stench. The complacency of the animal astounded me. It even urinated as I stood there and then proceeded to keep grazing. I was extremely glad to see the "no hunting" signs a little further down the trail.

Trail between Mile Marker 17 and 17.5 South

Allegheny River Trail South Mile Marker 17-17.5

Trying to document the trail as accurately as possible, I stopped again at mile marker 17. There was another deer right in front of me a little further up the trail. It grazed on the tender sprouts at the right edge of the trail, as I sat there not wanting to proceed in fear that I would disturb it. It watched as I wrote down the notes for this part of the guide. After standing there for quite a few minutes and seeing how fearless the peaceful creature was, I decided to reach into my backpack for my water bottle and relieve my thirst. I assumed this movement would scare it away. To my surprise, the deer just kept grazing, and started to walk towards me. It then stopped and proceeded to feed from the other side of the trail until it had its fill and slowly walked off into the woods.

Trail at northern entrance to St. George

Allegheny River Trail South Mile Marker 17.5-18.5

At approximately mile marker 17.5, the trail winds through a tiny, peaceful, river village called St. George. Like many of the river communities that this trail takes you through, the areas to the right and left of the trail are all private property. The picnic tables, benches, etc. are not part of the trail association property and the residence's privacy should be respected.

As you leave the quiet little village, a stream flows year round off to your left. The trail becomes cool and shady at this point and is a gorgeous ride.

Mile Marker 18.5 South

Allegheny River Trail South Mile Marker 18.5-19

On the right just past mile marker 18.5, you will discover a mowed clearing. It is an inviting place but is clearly marked private property. Do not take this path down to the river. If you proceed a little further down the trail, you will find a waterfall off to your left and then you will come upon a picnic table where you can rest or have lunch. It does not offer an excellent river view, but it sits in a very quiet setting in dense woods.

Picnic Area between Mile Marker 19 and 19.5 South

Allegheny River Trail South Mile Marker 19-19.5

Between mile marker 19 and mile marker 19.5, you will find a very nice picnic area. The clearing has a gravel bed which retards weed growth, and it has a trail that leads down to the river.

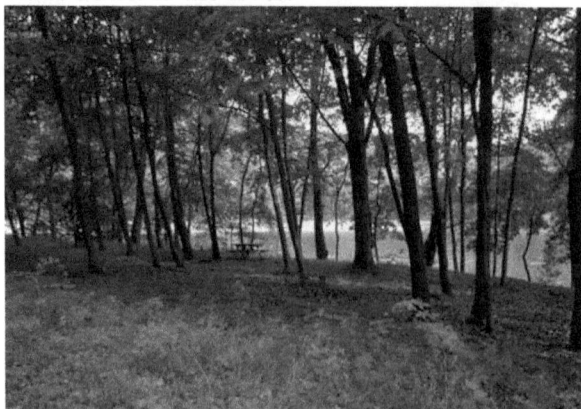

Campsite and Picnic Area between Mile Marker 19.5 and 20 South

Allegheny River Trail South Mile Marker 19.5-20

There is a camping area located here that is one of my favorite places to stop when I ride this section of the trail. The first time that I stopped here, I did it with Dakota. We ate lunch here, and I remember how delicious the food tasted. There is something about eating outdoors that always makes the food taste better.

This spot offers a lot more than a picnic area though. It hosts two fire rings and has ample level spots for tents. It also has a nice picnic table that offers a great view of the river. Watch the ridgeline above the opposite bank here. I usually see an eagle souring at this spot when a breeze kicks up.

One of the first times that I visited this tranquil spot, I spotted two deer walking in the woods across the trail. They ignored my camera shutter and bedded down right in front of me. The last time that I was there, I spotted an eagle on both legs of my trip.

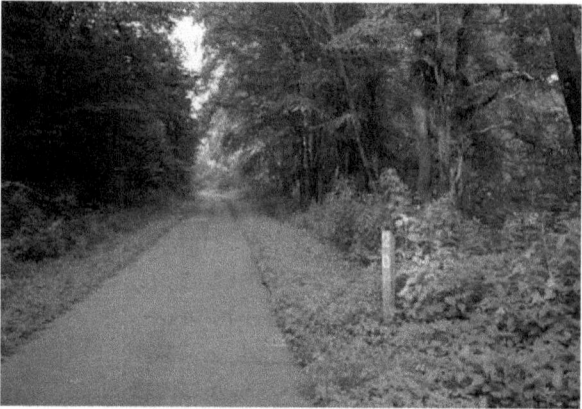

Mile Marker 20 South

Allegheny River Trail Mile Marker 20-20.5

Along this section of the trail, the riding experience is enhanced by nature's beauty: large ferns cover the riverbank and huge, old growth trees line the paved path. Although most of the trail along the Allegheny River is covered by a dense canopy, they are not old growth trees for the most part. Logging did away with most of the old growth trees. Only trees that had deformities and would not make good lumber at the time remain today.

Campsite between Mile Marker 20 and 20.5

Downstream from mile marker 20, you will find a trail leading down to the river. It offers a camping area with fire ring and a trail to the water, but sometimes it can be a bit overgrown and intimidating.

If you proceed a little further, you will find another camping area off to the right. It also has a fire ring and a trail to the water. Usually this path is less overgrown and is probably a better camping spot.

Right before you get to mile marker 20.5, from the left, you will hear a babbling waterfall. It only becomes rapid right after a storm, but the soothing sound of the water enhances the experience when passing through this section.

Mile Marker 20.5 South

Allegheny River Trail Mile Marker 20.5-21

At mile marker 20.5, the thick shady canopy from the trees clears and displays an awesome view of the bend in the river. There is a gas pipeline on the left, and a huge clearing that leads up the steep wall of the river valley. There is a clearing for the pipeline, and a path that goes down the center suggests that it is a route regularly used by bear or deer. Black bear tend to be territorial, and they will take the same trail repeatedly stepping in the exact spot they stepped before. Because of the wear of the trail, it could be a black bear crossing.

There are blackberry bushes on the right of the trail. These berries are favorites for many species of wildlife including black bear. Although there are black bears in this area, they are highly elusive during the day. You will probably never see one unless you venture out extremely early in the morning or late into the evening.

Generally, when possible, black bears will run or avoid humans. If you see one though, leave the area immediately just in case. The word "wild" is in wildlife for a reason. Any type of wildlife is highly unpredictable, and a black bear with cubs is extremely dangerous.

It is common to see fawns and other baby wildlife on the trails. Many people make the mistake of thinking that its mother abandoned it. This is most often far from the case. If you spot a baby, you can guarantee the mother is nearby. Leave the baby alone. It does not need rescued, and never try to pet a wild animal.

Kits --- baby foxes --- are often spotted on the trail and seem completely unafraid of humans. Please stay away from them. If they become accustomed to human contact, they will be vulnerable as an easy target for hunters.

Most wildlife will never approach a human. If they do, always be extremely leery and get away from it. There are reported cases of rabies in raccoons through the counties the trail encompass. Most mammals can contract rabies if bitten. Even a baby kit could have rabies.

As you proceed toward mile marker 21, you will hear a waterfall off to your left. It is difficult to see, but again, the sound of the rushing water just makes the ride more enjoyable.

A bit further down the trail, on the right, you will find a nice camping area with a fire ring and a flat spot very close to the river. It is close enough to Rockland Station for easy emergency exit, too.

Freedom Falls

Before you get to mile marker 21, Rockland Station Road greets you on the left. Take Rockland Station Road up the hill about a quarter of a mile, and on the right, there is a well-worn path down to a gorgeous waterfall called Freedom Falls.

Historic Rockand Iron Furnace

Taking a walk just a few hundred yards below reveals an amazing sight as well as an interesting piece of local history. The remains of the Rockland Furnace stand here. It is well-preserved considering it originated in 1832. Before the discovery of oil in Titusville, the entire area flourished from the rich blessings of iron ore. Communities were built around similar iron furnaces. These towns, however, have long since disappeared. This iron furnace is a great way to experience local history from the great mineral wealth of the area, and Freedom Falls is a majestic place to experience for its natural beauty.

There are several fire pits in this area, and it looks as if the site is well-used for camping. At the end of Rockland Station Road, there is ample parking. This is a wonderful area to park, camp, and take a day or two to absorb. The wildlife is abundant, the beauty is never ending, and you can almost taste the history around you!

Parking Area at Northern Entrance to Rockand Tunnel

Allegheny River Trail Mile Marker 21-22

Mile marker 21 is located at the north end of the Rockland (Woodhill) Tunnel. Across from the mile marker marker are two plaques. One provides information about the Rockland Furnace. It discusses the origin, the operation, and the dangers that were involved for the workers.

Next to it is a plaque that discusses the Rockland (Woodhill) Tunnel. The construction of this tunnel, as with the Kennerdell tunnel, was a great engineering feat in its day. It was built in 1916 by using huge steam shovels to excavate through the rocky expanses. These tunnels were built by the Allegheny Valley Railroad to reduce the distance of traveling along the curvy Allegheny River to Pittsburgh.

Southern Entrance to Rockland Tunnel

The Rockland (Woodhill) Tunnel

This tunnel is not as long as the Kennerdell Tunnel, but it can seem just as ominous when passing through it. Like all three tunnels on the Allegheny Valley Rails to Trails system, a flashlight is required to pass through safely. Make sure your batteries are charged. I once passed through this tunnel with a dim flashlight, and I could not see in front of my face, much less where I was stepping.

In all the tunnels, the Trail Association highly recommends walking your bicycle through them instead of riding. These tunnels are so dark and formidable that it is easy to become disorientated. When you cannot see the ground, it is extremely difficult to keep your balance in these tunnels, and accidents occur. In addition, the reflectors in the middle of the trail and on the sides tend to put a rider into a sort of trance. They flash at you constantly in good light when you pedal through.

The last time that I walked through this tunnel, two young men passed me on my way out. I warned them about riding through the tunnel on their bikes, and they kindly laughed me off and continued. Within a minute or two, I heard "Whoa!", as one of them slid off the paved trail into the gravel that line the banks of the dark deep tunnel.

When you approach the south end of the tunnel, in most seasons, you will encounter dripping water. Before passing through, make sure you tuck all cameras, etc. away to protect them because they might get wet.

At the south entrance to the tunnel, there is a camping area with fire ring and picnic table. In spring and after it rains, water drips from the steep cliffs to the left.

An unpaved trail leads off to the right of the entrance. This is a bypass for the tunnel, but I highly discourage anyone from using it. It is rough, usually muddy, and leads to a private road through Rockland Station. Some people in this small village resent bicycling through their village. They are not too friendly, and this detour actually takes you about three more miles than riding through the tunnel.

Allegheny River Trail Mile Marker 22-22.5

There are no mile markers between mile marker 21 and 22.5. At approximately mile 22, on your left, you will see a small waterfall surrounded by blackberry bushes. As you proceed further, you will see the remains of an old oil tank --- yet another reminder of the area's oil history that these trails provide.

Clearing between Mile Marker 22.5 and 23 South

Allegheny River Trail Mile Marker 22.5-23

Just past mile marker 22.5, there is another huge gas line clearing on the left.

Many people do not realize it, but our area is also rich in natural gas. Some of the first gas wells were drilled in this region. Like the other gas line clearing on this section of trail, it has a well-worn patch down the steep hillside and a path that leads down to the river. No doubt that this is some type of animal crossing.

The blackberry bushes and choke cherry bushes that line this part of the trail attract many forms of wildlife. This is a bird watcher's paradise. The river and trees offer great nesting advantages, and during migration times, wide varieties of species use it as their corridor.

Beaver on the Allegheny River

There are signs of beavers along this stretch, too. Beaver are abundant along the Allegheny River. They are nocturnal for the most part, so you usually will not see one during the day. Late in the evenings, though, the beavers emerge from their dens to feed, play, and swim the mighty river.

Most of the beavers in this area along the river do not build the customary dams found inland. Instead, they build their dens in the banks of the river. Because of this behavior, people often refer to them as "bank beaver."

A great way to see beaver is to ride in the evening and listen to the water. Beavers usually smack their tails on the water to warn other beavers that danger is near. This is a very distinct sound and hard to miss if you listen closely.

On the left, a little further down, is an orange-colored waterfall. This waterfall, like many in our area, contains iron and thus the rocks and water possess the characteristic dark orange tint.

Mile Marker 23 South

Allegheny River Trail Mile Marker 23-23.5

There is a vast variety of birds along the Allegheny Trail. At mile marker 23, I spotted a Rose-Breasted Grosbeak. I am an avid bird watcher, and I have only spotted this type of bird a few times in my many rides and hikes through the years. Bird books say they are common, but I have not found that to be the case. Their beauty is astounding. They are black with some white in their wings and have a red and white breast. I always feel blessed when I see something so rare for me. This system of trails provides many such opportunities; there seems to be a blessing around every magnificent bend in this vast river valley.

There is a nice bench with a beautiful view of the river between mile marker 23 and 23.5. Spend a little time sitting here, and you can spot many varieties of wildlife. The red winged blackbirds are abundant here, and watch out for the kamikaze chipmunks. They tend to think it is a game to run out in front of a bicycle.

Historic Old RR Bridges over Mill Creek

Dotters Eddy

Passing through this section, you will find a clearing off to the left surrounded by a guardrail. This spot is Dotters Eddy. It is a gorgeous camping spot, and it hosts old railroad bridges. It also has a spillway that offers great wildlife spotting if you take the path down on the right from the trail.

A new wildlife viewing platform and camping area is in place at this point. The Allegheny Valley Conservancy project recently restored this area after it was almost destroyed by 4-wheeler traffic.

Allegheny River Trail Mile Marker 23.5-24

There is a deep valley to the left as you proceed through this section. Ferns line the valley before the steep cliffs of the riverbank. Deer are abundant here, and if you are quiet on the trail, you will see a lot of them in this location in the evenings.

Allegheny River Trail Mile Marker 24-24.5

Huge jagged cliffs covered with moss, ferns, and saplings that root themselves into the limited soil among the vast crevasses line the left side of the trail here.

At this point, you will begin to see private camps built along the trail. It is only about three miles from here to Emlenton. The camps are remotely located and often uninhabited on weekdays. They are private property and should be respected as such. The houses, though, do not take away from the ride. There is still plenty of wildlife and beautiful scenes to encounter.

Mile Marker 24.5 South
Allegheny River Trail Mile Marker 24.5-25

Just past mile marker 24.5, you come to a bridge going over Mill Creek. It has a view of an old railroad bridge built in 1912 that is no longer in use. This is a great spot to absorb the sounds of flowing water as it passes below you and continues out into the Allegheny River.

Just beyond the bridge is the Dotter Eddy Parking lot. You can reach this camping spot and parking area from Dotter Road by going up the hill in Emlenton and taking the left on to Dotter Road. It is unpaved and a bit rough, but if you drive slowly, it can be a great spot to spend a few days without having to pack all your camping gear in and out.

This spot houses a new canoe and kayak access launch making a good half-day trip from Franklin or a nice midway stop for a full day trip.

Allegheny River Trail Mile Marker 25-25.5

There is a bench with a scenic overlook just past mile marker 25. You will find an abundance of gray and red squirrel along all sections of the Allegheny River Trail. Reports say that the black-phase gray squirrel has a nesting place in this vicinity. Reports say that one in every 10,000 gray squirrels has a pigment mutation that gives it this color. In addition, some reports say that in the 1700-1800's all the squirrels in the area were black. Their fur was a precious commodity then because the dark pigmentation added extra warmth.

A bit further down on the right, there is a camping area. It offers a river view, and is not far from Emlenton if you want to pack in and out easily.

Allegheny River Trail Mile Marker 25.5-26

This stretch of trail offers great sound effects. The grassy peninsulas and rocky shorelines along the river cause a riffling, which provides the trail user a wonderful blend of bird songs and water. Look for scarlet tanagers here. Although they are not reportedly a rare bird in this area, they are seldom spotted and a beautiful sight to see. They are mostly all red with black wings and tail feathers. The colors stand out vividly in this dense canopy.

Allegheny River Trail Mile Marker 26-26.5

Between these two mile markers, there is a bench with a nice view of the Allegheny River. It is a nice resting place before you go into Emlenton and on the way north.

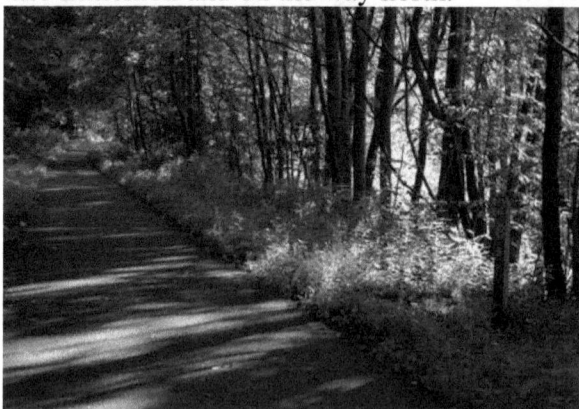

Mile Marker 26.5 South

Allegheny River Trail Mile Marker 26.5-27

As you proceed through this section of the trail, wildflowers are in abundance as they are in most seasons all along of the Allegheny River trails system. On the left, cement remains of the old Quaker State Refinery begin to intermingle with the wildflowers. The canopy opens in this stretch, and the remnants of the oil boom splay out visually in front to you.

Trail between Mile Marker 26.5 and 27 South

Quaker State Oil Refinery Remains

Allegheny River Trail Mile Marker 27-Emlenton Trailhead

There are two plaques placed here by the Allegheny Valley Trails Association that explain how the Quaker State Oil Refinery came to this once bustling metropolis. It displays a picture taken back in 1892, which allows the viewer great insight into how vast this oil refinery once was.

The second plaque is detailed and illustrates where you are standing and what was there once. It also explains when and why the oil refinery shut down in 1980.

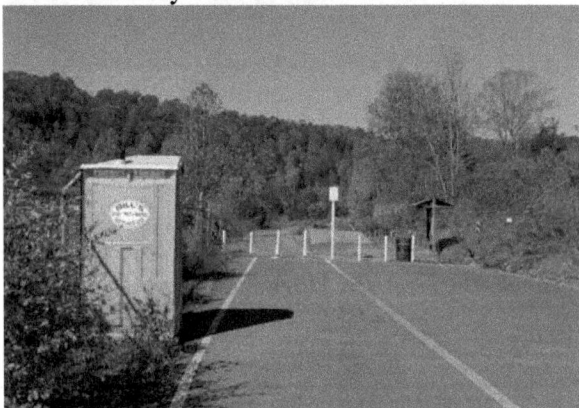

Emlenton Trailhead Parking Area

Allegheny River Trail Emlenton Trailhead

At the Emlenton trailhead, there is a gorgeous gazebo with a picnic table. It is a great place to rest, picnic, and offers bicycle racks. There is ample paved parking at this location and a porta potty.

Currently, this is the end of the Allegheny River Trail, but it picks up again in the town of Foxburg just down stream.

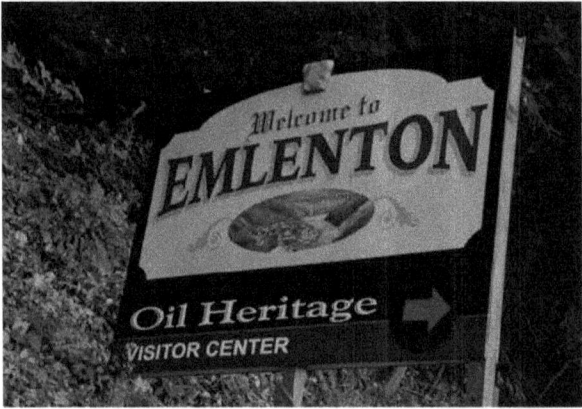

Emlenton

Emlenton is a small but beautiful little town located along the Allegheny River Trail. Current and past residents of this quaint area worked diligently to preserve the rich heritage passed down through the ages, and the historical architecture that survived tells much of the story of the town's eventful history.

Although many towns from the oil boom days disappeared into ghost towns, Emlenton survived and prospered without taking on the big city feel of some of the larger towns further north along the trail. Even before the days of commercial oil drilling, Emlenton prospered because of its convenient location along the Allegheny River and the vast lumber and iron resources that surround the area.

The trail leading into Emlenton is remote and abundant with wildlife, but venturing into this small town is a reward in itself. A great window into the past can be seen by just strolling down the quiet streets and absorbing the well-preserved historical structures that encompass the entire town. It seems that almost every building has a story.

The Crawford Center in Emlenton home of the Pumping Jack Museum

One of the best places to start your tour is at the Pumping Jack Museum. It is located in the Crawford Center, which at one time was the high school. While you are there, pick up a book titled, *A Stroll Through Historic Emlenton.* It is one of the best publications about the history of the town and the significance of all the old building that still stand in abundance.

Written in collaboration by Nancy Kingsley, Joanne Long, and Arch Newton, this publication literally leads you down the streets and lists the historical homes by the current address. This walking guide makes for the perfect tour. Along with old historical pictures of the buildings, it also discusses in-depth about the leading founders and developers that made the beautiful little town what it is today.

This comprehensive guide starts out by expertly summarizing the history of Emlenton within the inside cover. The authors of the work did such a good job of conveying the information that it made no sense to try to interpret it differently. The passages below come directly from *A Stroll Through Historic Emlenton.*

Synoptic History of Emlenton

Emlenton's first recorded settler was a squatter by the name of John Kerr. In approximately 1810, he cleared a small section and built a cabin on a site near the present bridge. He drowned while loading a flatboat with the building stones that were to be used in Pittsburgh. John Cochran came next, staying but a short time before removing to Richland Township. Then, prior to 1820, Andrew McCaslin, and enterprising young Irishman, poled up the Allegheny on a flatboat

*in search of building
stone. Enchanted with
the beauty of the
surrounding hills, he
bought property within
the area, which became
the borough of
Emlenton. Also of
importance to the
town's development,
families had begun to
locate in outlying areas
after 1798 when
Congress declared the
land open for settlement.*

*In no time,
McCaslin was joined by
other adventurous souls
and soon a wharf and
tavern were established,
creating a village. By
1834 homes were being
erected and lumbering
became a prosperous
business. By 1839
twenty iron furnaces
were in operation within
a sixteen-mile radius of
the new community from
which barges carried
pig iron downstream.*

*Emlenton
received its name from
Hannah Emlen, the wife
of Joseph Fox, a*

wealthy merchant from Philadelphia who owned vast acreage in both Venango and Clarion Counties. At the time the town was surveyed, Fox and McCaslin owned the entire town site and beyond. From a midline running roughly east to west, Fox owned land to the south and McCaslin to the north.

Emlenton soon became a trading center. The Kittanning Iron Works established the "Iron Store;" warehouses dotted the riverbank; a foundry began operation; hotels were built to accommodate the visitors and businessmen; and the Allegheny Valley Railroad built northward to town. By the time oil was first drilled in Titusville in 1859, Emlenton's leaders had developed a business sense. They communicated well with

*each other and worked
for the economic
development of the
community.*

    *An example of
the cooperative spirit
was the building of the
first Emlenton Bridge.
This wooden, covered
bridge was, at the time,
the only toll bridge
spanning the Allegheny
River in Venango
County. Although they
were living in a small
village, they had the
foresight to see the
advantages and promise
of such a project. By
1856 the bridge was
open for business.*

    *Soon "black
gold fever" radiated
southward and in 1867
Emlenton's first oil well
was drilled on Ritchey
Run. Emlenton became
the rail point for
receiving pipe and other
supplies for the area's
newly developed oil
fields. The Eagle Iron
Works moved here from
Brandon's Ferry and
became headquarters*

for machine and tool work. The E & C Bradley Company, an oil well supplier, of Olean, New York, located in town. James Bennett and John Porterfield made their fortunes selling oil well supplies.

A local group of men envisioned that "natural gas" could be harnessed as a reliable commercial lighting and fuel source. In 1882 the Emlenton Gas Light and Fuel Company was formed – the first organized natural gas company in Venango County, one of the first to be chartered in the stand the third such in the United States. This was the beginning of the Columbia Gas System.

Local oil producers banded together and in 1891 formed the Emlenton Producers Oil Company. In 1931 a merger among nineteen regional firms resulted

*in the formation of
Quaker State Oil
Refining Corporation, a
dominant influence in
the economic structure
of Emlenton for 60
years...*

A historical plaque marks the spot of the Oil Refinery as you enter into Emlenton from the Allegheny River Trail. It has pictures of how it looked, where it once stood, and it explains the layout of the plant in its prime.

Like many of the old structures that came about throughout the rich history of the town, the old Gas Company building still stands and now houses the local newspaper, *The Progress News*, and is home to Staab Typographic, the publisher of *A Stroll Through Historic Emlenton*.

The oldest building in town is also still standing and now houses Otto's Tavern. It is a nice place for a historical lunch in the area or some liquid refreshment while experiencing first hand part of Emlenton's rich history. Originally, according to Arch Newton, this building was a teahouse and the upstairs was used as a boarding house. The business has now been in the Schiberl family for over forty years, and they know all the ins and outs of entertaining. With daily food and drink specials and parties that last into the wee hours, this is one place that you will want to visit.

This town might be small, but the accommodations in and around the area are plentiful and the range of prices is sure to fit any budget. This area offers a wonderful five star hotel, the Foxburg Inn, located just a couple of miles south along the Allegheny River and has rooms that include fireplaces and Jacuzzi tubs that will satisfy even the fussiest traveler.

If you like camping, Gaslight Campground is located conveniently off I-80 and offers 120 full service hookups for RV camping, cabins, rustic camping spots, a brand new heated pool, mini golf, and much more. This is the nicest campground available along the trails and the owners, John and Martha Berry, are the perfect hosts for long term or short term camping adventures. They even offer bicycle rentals and a shuttle service down to the Allegheny River Trail.

The Barnard House is a bed and breakfast located in town. It is an historical, restored home that sits on the banks of the Allegheny River. Filled with antiques and old photographs of the Barnard family and with a wrap-around porch that faces the river, this is a unique and reasonably inexpensive place to stay while visiting this gorgeous area.

Mineral Springs

While you are in town, Mineral Springs is another spot you will not want to miss. Not only is it the site of the oldest working oil well in the world, the hike back to the spot and the surrounding area is gorgeous. Overnight rustic camping is free, but you need to call the borough building before hand so they do not close the gates. It usually is closed by dark unless there are campers there.

The Emlenton Mill Creamery is another great spot to visit while you are in the area. They have incredible ice cream, a hostel available for groups, free internet and computers, and the inside of the Mill is preserved with all the old working machinery still labeled and existing. Upstairs is the only antique shop in town.

While it might not be easily seen just glancing at Emlenton, this small town has a multitude of fun and historic places to visit and scenery that you won't want to miss; it definitely is one of the best central locations to explore all the trails.

Emlenton Canoe and Kayak Rentals

For canoeing or kayaking in the area, **Riverview Canoe** is the place to call to arrange your trip. The owner, Mike Berry, offers a wide range of trip options from Franklin down to Parker. There are even trips that last several days available all at extremely reasonable rates. This business has several vans to accommodate the largest to the smallest groups and the Old Town canoes and kayaks are top quality. To arrange your outing on the river, call 724-867-9480.

Emlenton Bicycle Rentals

Bicycle rentals are available at **Gaslight Campground**. They even offer a shuttle service for your convenience. You can contact them at 724-867-6981.

Emlenton Museums

Pumping Jack Museum
511 Hill Street
724-867-0300
(Call for an appointment)

Emlenton Camping

Gaslight Campground

6297 Emlenton Clintonville Rd.
724-867-6981
☐ HYPERLINK
"http://www.gaslightcampground.com"
☐www.gaslightcampground.com☐

Mineral Springs
Call the Borough Building for overnight rustic camping.
724-867-8611

Emlenton Hotels and Motels

Foxburg Inn
20 Main Street
724-659-3116
☐ HYPERLINK
"http://www.foxburginn.com"
☐www.foxburginn.com☐

Emlenton Motor Inn
6318 Emlenton Clintonville Road
(724) 867-2314

Emlenton Bed and Breakfast

The Barnard House Bed & Breakfast
108 River Avenue
724-8672261
☐ HYPERLINK
"http://www.thebarnardhouse.com"
☐www.thebarnardhouse.com☐

Emlenton Restaurants

Sue's Hometown Pizzaria
615 Main Street
724-867-0201

Plaza Restaurant
6406 Emlenton Clintonville Road
724-867-9171

Oil Rig Lunch Depot
511 Hill Street
724-867-5362

Otto's Tavern
611 River Road
724-867-0952

Emlenton Mill Creamery
201 Main Street
724-867-0277

Mike's Restaurant and Lounge
RR 3, Emlenton, PA
724-867-2298

Allegheny Grille
40 Main St. Foxburg
724-867-5701

<u>Emlenton Golf Courses</u>

Stoney Meadow Golf Course
Emlenton, PA
724-867-0067

Foxburg Country Club (Approximately 3 miles down river)
369 Harvey Road
Foxburg, PA 16036
724 659-3196

Foxburgh Information Center

Foxburg

As far as size is concerned, Foxburg is probably one of the smallest towns along the Allegheny River Trail, but do not let the population of this little metropolis deter you from visiting. It is rich in history and is the ultimate destination for the visitor who prefers to be pampered with five star luxuries.

Originally, this town and all of the Commonwealth of Pennsylvania were given to William Penn from the king of England, Charles II back in 1681. At that time and for many years afterwards, early settlers considered this western part of the state as the "Wild West." During the years after this land was granted to William Penn, mostly only Native Americans inhabited the area.

The story goes that William Penn owed Samuel Mickle Fox a favor of some sort and agreed to give him land to settle the debt. According to all reports, Penn offered Fox as much land as one man could walk in a day. Fox was a smart businessperson, but realized he probably could not walk too far through such a wild and untamed territory, so he came up with the incredibly smart idea of hiring the fastest Native American brave in the area to do the traversing for him. On the longest day of the year, that brave started out and walked an unbelievable distance that encompassed approximately 1100 acres. Mostly all of this land stood along the Allegheny River from the mouth of the Clarion River and northward.

Samuel Mickle Fox worked as a banker in Philadelphia, and reports state that he never settled the untamed properties of his estate, but his son, Joseph Mickle Fox, built a summer home for his new wife, Hanna Emlen, and himself on the hill where the two great waterways, the Clarion River, (then called Toby Creek) and the Allegheny River met. The couple having married in 1820, the construction of their new summer home, which was made from natural materials obtained on the estate property, was completed in 1828.

However, it was not until 1847 that Joseph Mickle Fox made Foxburg a town, and soon after, his many accomplishments for the town had a lasting impact, and several of the buildings he had built then, still stand today. He was a philanthropist and contributed greatly to the entire community.

According to the Foxburg Free Library website at □ HYPERLINK "http://www.csonline.net/foxburglibrary/local_history3.htm"

, once the first commercial oil well was discovered in Titusville, the small town of Foxburg boomed from its small population of 100 people to 10,000 people almost overnight. The main reason for this extraordinary growth was the location between the two rivers and Foxburg's central location and connection to many of the outer lying towns where black gold fever ran rampant with the many highly producing wells that dotted the entire landscape.

Once the fever spread to other states where bigger wells were drilled and discovered, Joseph M. Fox continued his building of the fashionable little town by bringing the sport of golf to the area. The course began with just three holes in a cow pasture, but it now stands as the Foxburg Country Club, which houses the Golf Hall of Fame, and a challenging 9 hole golf course open to the public. It is considered to be the golf course with the longest record of continuous use in the United States.

Fox's contributions to the town still did not stop there, though. In 1882, he erected a gorgeous Episcopal church on the hill above Foxburg and near the golf course and dedicated it to his community. The church still stands today and is an architectural marvel.

In 1910, Fox went even further to help his community by building the Foxburg Free Library. This building, made of all local flagstones, continues to stand today, and the library is still free to the public.

The Fox estate now is private property, but the owners continue following Joseph Fox's generous footsteps. Although Foxburg's old inn and restaurant disappeared years ago, new ones were built in their place. Looking at old photographs, it appears the builders tried to make the new building as similar as possible to the originals, while offering all the modern comforts anyone would desire. The Foxburg Inn is situated directly on the banks of the Allegheny River, and most of the rooms offer breathtaking views along with Jacuzzi tubs and many more amenities.

Across the street from the hotel is the Foxburg Wine Cellars. They offer free wine tasting daily and produce some of the most delicious local wines in Pennsylvania. Although not recommended for before a trek out on the bike trail, this is a great place to stop and sit outdoors after a long day on the trail to soak in the opulent beauty that surrounds this picturesque little town on the Allegheny River.

If you are hungry, the Allegheny Grille is located next door to the hotel and offers many entertainment opportunities along with outstanding food sure to satisfy any palette. On the other side of the Foxburg Inn are Foxburg Pizza and the Country Store. In addition to preparing some of the best pizza around, they also serve breakfast, lunch and dinner for your convenience.

With an art gallery, The Red Brick, a boutique, and horse drawn carriage tours (arrangements made at the Foxburg Wine Cellars), this is one trail town you will not want to pass up. Whether you spend just a day or visit for a week, this magnificent little town offers something for everyone's pleasure.

Foxburg Area Canoe and Kayak Rentals

Riverview Canoe
Yep Yep Blvd.
Emlenton, PA 16373
724-867-9480

Foxburg Area Bicycle Rentals

Segway of Western PA (Offers various tours on a Segway in and around Foxburg)
8 Main Street
Foxburg, PA 16036
724-659-0094
☐ HYPERLINK
"http://www.segwaywpa.com"
☐http://www.segwaywpa.com☐

Gaslight Campground
6297 Emlenton Clintonville Rd.
724-867-6981
☐ HYPERLINK
"http://www.gaslightcampground.com"
☐www.gaslightcampground.com☐

Foxburg Area Bed and Breakfast

The Barnard House Bed & Breakfast

108 River Avenue
724-8672261
☐ HYPERLINK
"http://www.thebarnardhouse.com"
☐www.thebarnardhouse.com☐

Foxburg Area Camping

Gaslight Campground
6297 Emlenton Clintonville Rd.
724-867-6981
☐ HYPERLINK
"http://www.gaslightcampground.com"
☐www.gaslightcampground.com☐

Mineral Springs
Call the Borough Building for overnight rustic
camping.
724-867-8611

Foxburg Area Hotel and Motels

*Foxburg Inn on the Allegheny an excellent
hotel choice in the area.*
Foxburg Inn

20 Main Street
724-659-3116
☐ HYPERLINK
"http://www.foxburginn.com"
☐www.foxburginn.com☐

Emlenton Motor Inn
6318 Emlenton Clintonville Road
(724) 867-2314

Foxburg Area Restaurants

The Allegheny Grille
40 Main Street
Foxburg, PA 16036
724-659-5701
☐ HYPERLINK
"http://www.visitfoxburg.com/"
☐http://www.visitfoxburg.com/☐

Foxburg Pizza and Country Store
12 Main Street
Foxburg, PA 16036
724-659-0122

Sue's Hometown Pizzaria
615 Main Street
724-867-0201

Plaza Restaurant
6406 Emlenton Clintonville Road
724-867-9171

Oil Rig Lunch Depot
511 Hill Street

724-867-5362

Otto's Tavern
611 River Road
724-867-0952

Emlenton Mill Creamery
201 Main Street
724-867-0277

Mike's Restaurant and Lounge
RR 3, Emlenton, PA
724-867-2298

Foxburg Area Golf Courses

Stoney Meadow Golf Course
Emlenton, PA
724-867-0067

Foxburg Country Club
369 Harvey Road
Foxburg, PA 16036
724 659-3196
☐ HYPERLINK
"http://www.foxburggolf.com/"
☐http://www.foxburggolf.com/☐

Foxburg Area Tours

Segway of Western PA
8 Main Street
Foxburg, PA 16036
724-659-0094

□ HYPERLINK
"http://www.segwaywpa.com"
□http://www.segwaywpa.com□

Riverstone Carriage Tours (Horse and Carriage Tours offered daily with reservations)
65 Main Street
Foxburg, PA 16036
724-659-0021
□ HYPERLINK
"http://www.foxburgwine.com/riverstone_carri age_tours"
□http://www.foxburgwine.com/riverstone_car riage_tours□

Foxburg Other Attractions

Divani Chocolate Boutique
22 N Palmer Ave
Foxburg, PA 16036
724-659-3146
http://www.divanichocolate.com/

Foxburg Wine Cellars offering free wine tasting.

Foxburg Wine Cellars
65 Main Street
Foxburg, PA 16036
724-659-0021
http://www.foxburgwine.com/

View of Clarion River from the Clarion River Bridge along this gorgeous stretch of trail.

The Foxburg - Parker Trail

Although this section is one of the shortest treks along the trail, it is well worth the trip and provides a rewarding jaunt. Most of this trail follows the river along the edge of the old Fox estate which is now called Riverstone Farm. Because this had been private land for many years, the wildlife is abundant. The trail is paved and level which makes it an easy ride for all members of the family. With many outdoor activities available in Foxburg and Parker, this is a great place to start or end your vacation in the area.

Across the river from the trail is a major, heavily-traveled road, and that does cause some road noise to be heard while using the trail, but it does not deter the wildlife from frequenting the area. Bald eagles are abundant along this stretch of trail, and this is one of the very few places where you can spot ospreys in

Pennsylvania. The waters of the mighty Allegheny River attract a wide variety of waterfowl, too. Wood ducks, which at one time were almost completely extinct in the area, are common along these boulder-lined banks.

About midway through the trail when traveling either south or north, the Clarion River Bridge carries you over the Clarion River. There is a blue heron rookery along the Stump Creek Island in the center of the Allegheny River almost directly across from this bridge. It is located up in sycamore tree, and the white bark of the tree makes it easy to locate. The nests are abundant, too.

There are a couple of different spots along the trail where you can enjoy primitive camping, and this entire section of trail is a segment of the North Country Trail. This is a great place to pick up this trail if you like hiking. At Parker, the North Country Trail crosses over the bridge and goes up the steep hill from the Parker Flat. The trail leads you across Bear Creek, and the bridges, wildlife, and pristine Pennsylvania woodlands give you a good feel of the longest trail in the United States.

At the south end of the trail lies another attraction: Indian Rock or Devil's Rock to some historians. It is a gorgeous rock formation with an amazing view of the river to the north or south. At the rock's top is a window-like opening through which the great expanse of the river valley is seen. It does not take a great imagination to realize what this rock was used for by the Native Americans or why it got its name. The rock stands tall along the eastern bank of the Allegheny and makes a great vantage point for seeing what is coming up or down the river. Be forewarned, though: hiking up to this rock is very dangerous. In summer, the steep and perilous route is surrounded by thick brush and the trail is almost completely obscured. If you decide to make the climb, be extremely careful because footholds are not solid, and the rocky terrain is great habitat for snakes --- some of which are poisonous --- so watch where you place your hands and feet.

Near the paved trail are a primitive camping spot and also a picnic table. The sounds of a small stream will also greet you. Indian Rock is located just before the Parker parking area when you are heading south. This spot is also the location of Parker's Landing which in the days of the oil boom produced a great amount of oil. The parking area does not offer any type of bathroom facilities, but there is a lot of space for parking, and it is a great place to start or stop your adventures along the Allegheny Valley Trails.

Foxburg Parking Area

Parking for this section of trail is ample. The Foxburg Visitor's Center is located at the trailhead in an old red caboose; this is a great place to stop for more information on the trail, attractions in the area, and upcoming events. The people here all work on a volunteer basis and they are warm, friendly, and informative.

The Foxburg - Parker Trail Mile Marker 0-.5 South

Starting out on the trail, there is a sewage treatment plant on the west side of the trail. Renovations are occurring at the plant, but it does not hinder one using the trail. During any construction, the paved trail is converted into a sand track that can be soft in places. But within a quarter mile, you are completely through this section, and the remoteness of the trail soon engulfs you.

This section of trail leads you along the lower edge of the old Fox estate which is now referred to as Riverstone Farm. As you begin the trail, the reason why the owners named it "Riverstone" soon becomes apparent. Massive boulders, some the size of a small house, line the river side and the steep wooded hillside to the east.

If you want to see wildlife along the trail, the best time to go is in the early mornings or in the evenings. I spotted baby raccoons right in the parking area one evening. Bald eagles nest around this starting point, too and are almost a common sight all along this stretch.

The bank of the river gorge rises steeply on the east side of the trail through this section. Mountain laurels and hardwood trees intermingle along the route heading south.

The decaying wood from old telephone poles still stand sporadically along the eastern side of the trail here, and they provide a haven for a wide variety of woodpeckers. Pilated Woodpeckers, Downy Woodpeckers, and red-throated woodpeckers are common throughout this woodland area as are many rare and migrating birds in early spring and late fall. Look to these old telephone poles, and you will get a treat if you enjoy spotting any woodpecker species.

Along this first section of the trail there are several locations where you can traverse down to the river. Huge boulders line the river and allow you to almost get on the fast flowing water. The trek down is dangerous and the river is usually moving rapidly, so if you consider venturing down to the river at this point, use extreme caution.

The Foxburg - Parker Trail Mile Marker .5-1 South

Just past mile marker .5, a small stream trickles under the paved path. It runs mostly in spring after the snow melts or anytime after a heavy rainstorm. Along the west side of the trail along the riverbank is an old stone foundation from a chimney and a rustic camping spot with a fire ring. There is a picnic table strategically placed here, too.

The remains of old metal oil containers, rusty pumps, and oil pipelines provide evidence of big oil's history along the trail here. Wells like this littered the entire section of trail between Foxburg and Parker during the oil boom.

Just south of this point, an old dilapidated shack still stands. I do not recommend venturing inside this unsafe structure. You never know what might be inside of this shack. Many animals use abandoned shelters like this for their homes. The roof looks completely unsound, and the floorboards will not hold weight.

Heading southward, hardwood trees mingle with mountain laurel and pines giving the trail a green look even in winter. In spring, the smell of the blooming mountain laurels greets you through this area.

An old stone foundation near a beautiful waterfall can be found along the eastern side of the trail. The water seems to run year round, and huge pines and mountain laurel line the water's steep decent. If you decide to go off the trail and investigate either of these sights, use caution and watch where you step.

Just south of this point is a private dirt road that leads up to Riverstone Farm. Like the many points of private property along the huge expanse of trail systems in this guide, I ask that you respect the property owners by not trespassing on this road.

As you proceed to the south, Stump Creek Island comes into view on the west side of the trail. Once oil wells started producing along the river on this route, two men, O. E. Shannon and William Hartley decided to erect oil derricks there in spite of the fact that the island is known to flood. Their gamble paid off and this site, which is approximately a mile north of Parker, added to the success of the huge Parker field of oil.

Today, a wide variety of waterfowl, migrating birds, and sandpipers take to the shallow shores. There is also an osprey platform at the southern tip of this island. Currently it does not hold a nest, but ospreys are spotted here frequently.

A water pipe feeds clear water off the steep bank on the eastern side of the trail located along this part of the trail. Reportedly, it is clean spring water. Like all water along the trail, though, it is best to use purification tablets if you intend to use it. If you are camping at the primitive camping area just before this point though, it makes a great place to wash up or refresh your camp water supply.

About two hundred yards before mile marker 1, coming from the hillside and enhancing one's passage through this area will be the sound of another stream that passes under the trail to empty into the Allegheny River.

The Foxburg - Parker Trail Mile Marker 1-1.5 South

Just before and right after mile marker 1 are small streams that feed into the river. The babbling decent and gushing drop down into the river gives this point in the trail a very peaceful feeling. A variety of bird calls enhance and mix with the sound of the streams making an audible menagerie.

Stump Creek Island is in full view on the west side of the trail here, and you will find the entire stretch of trail well-used. The people along the trail are friendly, and everyone that I encountered enjoyed telling the tales of what the adventure brought to them that day.

Huge boulders line the steep banks of the river along this point. They interrupt the fast flow of the Allegheny and offer a rippling effect in the river. Wood ducks, Merganser, Canada Geese, and a wide variety of other waterfowl use this area for nesting. Keep an eye on the shore here because river otter frequent the banks.

Stone Bench

On the eastern side of the trail is another water pipe that offers clear water. There is a stone bench here, and this is a nice spot to rest and observe the wildlife along the trail. The great honking of Canada geese often accompanies the sound of the flowing water at this resting point. The last time I was through the area, I spotted three wood ducks along the bank of the river here.

The remnants of the old oil pipeline can be seen along the eastern side of the trail as you head further southward, and the Clarion River Bridge that crosses over the Clarion River looms into view. Immediately before you cross the bridge, a path leads down to the Clarion River. It is to the east, and just by looking up the rocky Clarion River, you can see how remote this section of trail actually is. The huge second and third growth trees continue interrupted for as far as the eye can see on this side of the river.

Fishermen in Winter

I took a hike to this point one January and came upon some anglers out on the shallow rocky waters of the Clarion River. It was a cold day and the river was still full of huge icebergs. I knew I was crazy to hike alone at that time of year, but as soon as I saw those men out fishing in it, I felt rather sane.

However, I could not help but make a comment questioning their sanity as I called to them from the quiet but treacherous riverbank. They laughed and completely agreed that they were a bit crazy about fishing.

I asked them if they had spotted any wildlife that day. They quickly reported spotting two eagles fighting and diving at each other. I smiled and tried not to laugh as I informed them that January and February are the months that bald eagles mated. Several times that day, I saw the same eagles circling high above me as they called out to each other in a shrill high pitched scream that is very distinctive and amazing to hear.

The Foxburg - Parker Trail Mile Marker 1.5-2 South

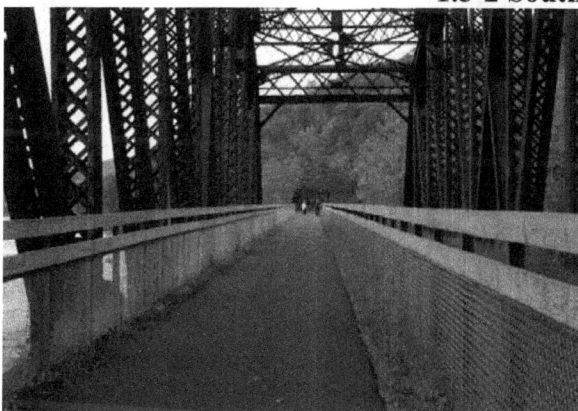

Trail on Clarion Bridge

Mile marker 1.5 south sits almost in the middle of the Clarion River Bridge. The bridge is fenced off to prevent mishaps, and even if you are a bit afraid of heights like I am, it is not intimidating to cross. It does offer some magnificent views, though. White-tailed deer are abundant along the banks of the Clarion River looking eastward, and spotting them is easy in early morning or evenings. This is also a great place from which to watch the sunset. The darkness arrives gradually along the river, and because this is a short trail, it is still easy to get out before dark.

Blue Heron Rookery on Stump Island

Across the river and a bit north, there is a huge sycamore tree with a number of nests in it. Originally a rookery for great blue heron, ospreys are reported also to nest here. The reason might be that this makes a great diving spot for these incredible birds of prey.

Once you cross over the bridge, the eastern side of the trail is not as steep and several four-wheeler trails lead off it. Because there are no motor vehicles allowed along the trail, they are not frequently used. They lead to private property, and the trail user should not be tempted to explore here.

The bank of the river on the western side of the trail is steep along here. You might not be able to get down to the river, but look to the shoreline, because it is usually a treat. Since this property along with the old Fox estate remained privately owned for more than a century, this entire area is abundant with wildlife. Bobcats, raccoon, opossum, and bear are just a few of the indigenous animals that take refuge in low traffic areas like this. Bobcats and black bears are mostly reclusive animals. If you spot one along the route, consider it a big treat. They might reside here, but seeing either is extremely rare.

Mile Marker 2.0

The Foxburg - Parker Trail Mile Marker 2-2.5 South

Proceeding through this last half mile of trail, the Parker Bridge comes into view. The bank on the west drops steeply into the Allegheny River, and the woodland hillside to the east is cluttered with sharp cliffs where mountain laurel clings to the ledges and water seeps down over the green mossy outcroppings.

. . .

This is a pretty stretch of trail, and it is hard to imagine that at one time, it was highly populated. This area is Parker's Landing. During the oil boom, reports calculate the population of this tiny section to be approximately 20,000 people. Before the oil boom, it was constantly in use, too. At first, it was just a small river crossing, but it soon became a popular landing spot for ferries that commuted up and down the river. Lumber was the main export, and eventually a store was erected here.

Once oil wells emerged around the area, the population soared and houseboats lined the shores up and down the Allegheny River. This crossing to the village of Lawrenceburg, now known as Parker City, was reportedly a major hub in the oil industry for the entire area.

Today, few remains from the population explosion still exist. There is a dilapidated wooden platform on the west side of the river that almost marks the spot where the boat crossing actually was. The geological formation called Indian Rock still stands strong and proud against the eastern horizon, but what was once a thriving city now stands dormant and in decay with only old black and white photographs and newspaper articles of the time that witness to its one time success.

. . .

Parking Area at Parker

At mile marker 2.5 south, you are at the Parker Parking Area. There are no facilities at this parking area, but the city of Parker lies across the river and offers most amenities. There is a picnic table to the east side of the trail and a fire ring for rustic camping, and there is ample parking.

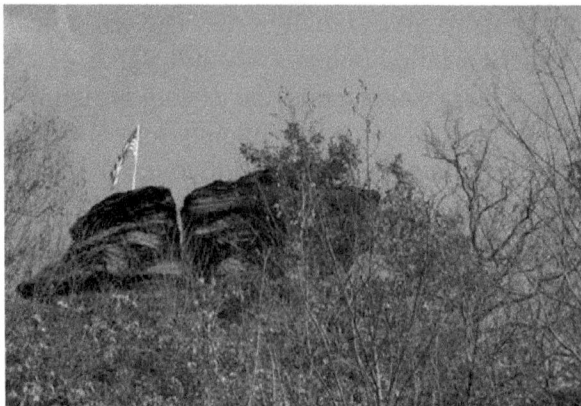

Indian Rock also known as Devil's Rock

      Indian Rock towers over this area. An American flag now stands upon its mighty crest. The white man once again lays claim to a sacred Native American spot. If you are thinking of hiking up to the peak, be extremely careful. The path is treacherous and the rock ledges are havens for reptiles.

Parker Bridge

Parker

After traversing south about 32 miles from its beginning, the paved Allegheny River Trail currently ends beneath the big blue inclined bridge that connects Armstrong and Clarion Counties at the city of Parker.

Located across the river from the trail, Parker's current appearance is merely a façade of its historic past when the town was heavily populated, economically prosperous, and was bustling with activity. Originally, of course, Native Americans inhabited the valley, and on the low-lying land along the river --- now, in Parker, designated as the "Flat" --- was an established Indian village. Peering down from the rocky cliffs --- particularly Indian Rock, a huge stone formation with a natural "eye" opening, and located just upstream of the Parker Bridge on the Clarion County (Trail side) bank of the Allegheny River --- the Indians reportedly peered down upon the

European intruders. Eventually, though, manifest destiny plowed through the region forever changing its cultural and physical landscape.

During the frenzy of the oil boom, the towns of Lawrenceburg (currently the "Bluff") and Parker's Landing (the "Flat" along the river) were, by special state legislation, incorporated as a city on March 1, 1873 with the new city taking the name of Parker thus forever honoring the original surveyor of the area, John Parker. At its inception, the city of Parker was home to over 20,000 people.

The economic boom of the oil industry, which included an Oil Exchange located on the Flat, lasted a mere decade and was over by the 1880s. Good fortune continued with the area's numerous pipe lines and the natural resources of iron ore and coal, but the closing of the glass factory one hundred years later, can sadly but arguably be considered the ultimate end of financial prosperity for the city. In the one hundred forty years since becoming a city, the number of businesses in Parker has steadily decreased, and today the survivors can be counted by fingers on two hands. Parker has, however, retained its city charter --- and thus accurately boasts the title of "The Smallest City in the United States. Currently fewer than 900 people live in Parker.

It should be noted here that Whittier, Alaska also claims to be the smallest city in the United States.

There is, however, a proud sense of community among Parker's friendly residents, and particularly as the last stop on the trail, Parker has many offerings for the adventurer. Along the river is a grocery store with gas pumps, restaurants and bars, places to rent bicycles and a place to rent canoes and kayaks. The Parker House Hotel, the oldest building in Parker, also offers inexpensive room rental over the bar and serves breakfast, lunch, and dinner.

Parker is also a good place to connect with the North Country Trail. Northward, this amazing hiking trail follows the Allegheny River Trail and southward, it takes you deep into the Pennsylvania woods toward Bear Creek. Soon to be the longest trail in the United States, this section gives the hiker/ backpacker/ camper a great taste of this pristine woodland while still allowing boasting that they hiked part of this history-making trail.

Recently Parker resident and local historian Marilyn McCall has published two fascinating books that provide a wealth of information about Parker. Her first book, *From Boom to Bust,* details the rise and fall of Parker when its economy was based on oil. Through Marilyn's interesting words, a reader will be introduced to significant people and families of Parker's history, and the commercial, cultural and historical changes that have taken place throughout the last century and a half are explained. She also presents a timeline marking significant events from 1748 through 2008. Along with the numerous photographs, charts, and illustrations that *From Boom to Bust* contains, Marilyn McCall's prose makes it not only a valuable source of historic information, but an interesting book to read. It is particularly intriguing to compare the historic photographs contained in the book with one's current view of specific sites.

Her second book, *Ben Hogan's Wild Ride* was recently published and describes the life of one of western Pennsylvania's most notorious "bad boys" who the author states called himself the both "the Man from Hell" and the "Wickedest Man in the World." His scandalous adventures along the river in Parker are sure to hold a reader's attention, and in spite of Ben Hogan's behaviors, his life story as explained by Marilyn McCall, holds valuable lessons for each of us.

Both of Marilyn McCall's books are available at numerous establishments along the trail.

Parker Canoe and Kayak Livery

For canoeing or kayaking in the area, **Riverview Canoe** is the place to call to arrange your trip. The owner, Mike Berry, offers a wide range of trip options from Franklin down to Parker. There are even trips that last several days available all at extremely reasonable rates. This business has several vans to accommodate the largest to the smallest groups and the Old Town canoes and kayaks are top quality. To arrange your outing on the river, call 724-867-9480.

Parker Bicycle Repairs and Rentals

Bicycle rentals are available at **Gaslight Campground**. They even offer a shuttle service for your convenience. You can contact them at 724-867-6981.

Happy Trails is located conveniently in Parker, but it does not offer bicycle rentals. They do minor bicycle repairs though and sell new bikes specializing in three wheel bicycles.
143 Washington Street
Parker, PA 16049
724-399-2721

Parker Camping

Gaslight Campground
6297 Emlenton Clintonville Rd.
724-867-6981
☐ HYPERLINK
"http://www.gaslightcampground.com"
☐www.gaslightcampground.com☐

Mineral Springs
Call the Borough Building for overnight rustic camping.
724-867-8611

Parker Hotel & Motels
Foxburg Inn

20 Main Street
724-659-3116
□ HYPERLINK
"http://www.foxburginn.com"
□www.foxburginn.com□

Emlenton Motor Inn
6318 Emlenton Clintonville Road
(724) 867-2314

Parker House Hotel
River Avenue
Parker, PA 16049
724-399-9911

Parker Bed & Breakfast
The Barnard House Bed & Breakfast
108 River Avenue
724-8672261
□ HYPERLINK
"http://www.thebarnardhouse.com"
□www.thebarnardhouse.com□

River Watch Bed and Breakfast
Bluff Avenue
Parker, PA 16049
724-399-4642

Parker Restaurants
Allegheny Grille
40 Main St. Foxburg
724-867-5701

Riverstone Lounge and Grill
208 N River Avenue
Parker, PA 16049
724-399-1100

Bob's Place Restaurant
103 N Wayne Avenue
Parker, PA 16049
724-399-4221 or 724-399-4268

Parker House Hotel
River Avenue
Parker, PA 16049
724-399-9911

Allegheny River Trail GPS Points

Northern Trailhead
N41°23.194
W079°49.106

Belmar Trailhead
N41°19.854
W079°49.896

Brandon Trailhead
N41°18.923
W079°51.159'

Indian God Rock
N41°17.547
W079°50.085

2 Picnic Tables and 1 Bench
N41°19.849
W079°49.503

Belmar Bridge and Sandy Creek Trail Intersection
N41°19.492
W079°47.327

Emlenton to Kennerdell Tunnel GPS Points

Crawford Center and Jumping Jack Museum
N41°29.218
W079°48.095

Emlenton Trailhead
N41°10.645
W079°48.095

Primitive Campsight w/fire ring but no picnic
N41°10.716
W079°42.945

Dotters Eddy Trailhead between mile marker 24&25
N41°12.641
W079°43.512

Dotters Eddy with spillway and scenic tunnels
N41°13.479
W079°43.377

Rockland Tunnel entrance and picnic table
N41°13.871
W079°44.406

Trailhead between Rockland and Kennerdell Trailheads
N41°13.886
W079°44.418

Path that leads to River: Great Picnic Area on River rocks
N41°13.92
W079°45.370

Primitive Camping Area w/ 2 fire rings
N41°13.892

W079°45.893

Primitive Camping on River w/ firering
N41°13.837
W079°45.994

Primitive Camping w/ 2 picnic tables
N41°13.613
W079°46.421

Picnic Table
N41°13.631
W079°46.419

Picnic Table
N41°14.388
W079°46.850

Covered Lean Two and picnic table
N41°16.100
W079°47.663

Picnic Table
N41°16.789
W079°48.589

Kennerdell Tunnel South Entrance
N41°16.789
W079°48.810

Saint George
N41°16.757
W079°48.811

What's To Come

The Allegheny Valley Trails Association constantly works to improve the trail system. In the most recent minutes from their meeting, they announced what is to come next along the trail. This is their list:

Emlenton to Foxburg
Saltbox Visitors Center
Clarion Highland Trail
Justus Trail
Parker to West Monterey

Notes

www.ingramcontent.com/pod-product-compliance
Lightning Source LLC
Chambersburg PA
CBHW070758100426
42742CB00012B/2185